Teaching that
Transforms

Teaching that Transforms

Why Anabaptist-Mennonite Education Matters

John D. Roth

Mennonite
Publishing
Network

Library of Congress Cataloging-in-Publication Data
Roth, John D., 1960- author.
  Teaching that transforms : why Anabaptist-Mennonite
education matters / John D. Roth.
      p. cm
  ISBN 978-0-8361-9552-1 (pbk. : alk. paper)
  1. Mennonites—Education. I. Title.
  LC586.M4R68 2011
  371.071'43—dc22
                                                    2010046028

16 15 14 13 12 11   10 9 8 7 6 5 4 3 2 1

To order or request information please call
1-800-245-7894 or visit www.heraldpress.com.

To my parents, Paul and Caroll June Roth, my first and best teachers, whose faithful support of Millersburg Mennonite Church and lifelong investment in Mennonite education have profoundly shaped my Christian life.

Contents

Foreword

I well remember the day I first met John Roth as a young history professor at Goshen College in October 1991. I was accompanying a new pastor at an orientation to Mennonite Church offices in Elkhart, so I joined the group that was invited to visit the denominational archives on the Goshen College campus. Walking toward the brick building, I overheard comments about how boring this event would be. That changed as soon as we met Roth, who was the host for the occasion. He began by showing us a couple of centuries-old books in his collection. We listened, enraptured, as he recounted the Mennonite story in a way that touched all members of our ethnically diverse group. It turned out that we lingered so long with engaged questions that we were late for the next scheduled "stop" on the tour.

A gifted teacher as well as an astute historian, Roth clearly demonstrated the truth of the adage that "there are no boring subjects, only boring teachers." Within a matter of minutes, Roth was able to transform our thinking about the nature and purpose of the church's historical archives. We came to see them not solely as a depository for old records, but rather as a rich repository of resources that can help us tell stories of God's faithfulness to God's people.

Since that day in Goshen, I've watched Roth exercise his considerable gifts as a teacher, writer, historian, and public speaker. The book you have in hand is but another example of his ability to communicate deep conviction with clarity, careful nuance, and grace. In the present volume, Roth not only discusses the history of the schools connected with Mennonite Education Agency, but does so in a way that will capture your attention as a reader.

He describes with empathy the sectarian impulses that led to the founding of many of the early Mennonite schools as a "defensive means of preserving a sociological and theological birthright." He goes on to describe their transformation into a more engaged and welcoming stance that has attracted students as well as teachers from beyond the Mennonite Church. He contends that this change is more than "a survival strategy in a competitive marketplace." Rather, he believes that "nurturing relationships with people beyond the traditional boundaries of the Mennonite community is a positive and consistent expression of the Anabaptist-Mennonite faith." He recognizes the value of a missional approach to the educational task, yet raises important questions about the way that mission is best carried out. With sensitivity to those who differ, Roth makes the case that there is still a vital place for distinctive Mennonite education.

At the behest of Mennonite Education Agency, Roth has produced in this volume an Anabaptist philosophy of education. If you anticipate a boring discussion on an abstract topic, you are in for a pleasant surprise. This book is infused with life and energy from Roth's conviction that Mennonite schools "will be shaped by a Christ-centered way of reading Scripture, a Christ-centered understanding of relationships with other people, and a Christ-centered view of the church as the visible form of the resurrected Jesus in the world today." Roth not only discusses the topic in a helpful manner; he provides vivid examples along the way.

This volume also takes a look at pedagogy—the practice or art of teaching—from an Anabaptist perspective. Again, with vivid examples, Roth demonstrates ways that effective Christian teaching cultivates in students an attentiveness to God's creative presence by encouraging the full expression of all the bodily senses. He contends that some of the most influential teaching in a Christian school is done outside of the planned curriculum in the classroom. The underlying ethos of a school—its philosophy, organizing assumptions, and daily practices—impact students as deeply as the teachers in the classroom. Particularly when there are inconsistencies between the stated mission and the actual practices of a school, more is "caught" than "taught."

One of the most helpful insights in this book is Roth's gentle insistence that there's no escaping the "embarrassment of particularity." By this, he means that every school, like every church, will always reflect a "*particular* theological and cultural identity.*" There is no such thing as a generic "Christian" institution. Therefore, Mennonite schools will do well to cultivate and openly express the distinctions that lie at the heart of their educational endeavor.

Like John Roth's family, all five members of my own family have enjoyed the educational benefits of a school affiliated with Mennonite Education Agency. Both my wife Bonnie and I graduated from Eastern Mennonite Seminary. Except for the year our family lived in Wales, all three of our children attended kindergarten through eighth grade at Kraybill Mennonite School in Mount Joy, Pennsylvania, and graduated from Eastern Mennonite University. We owe a debt of gratitude for the way these schools have shaped our lives.

Recently Bonnie and I enjoyed a stay of several days in John Roth's home. We joined John and his wife, Ruth, in conversations around the dining room and in the relaxed atmosphere of the living room. We conversed about a wide range of topics—our families, intimate participation in our local churches, meaningful work in church's institutions, and engagement with other Christians on the international scene. The Roths' warm hospitality confirmed what I sensed in John nearly twenty years ago—his participation in Mennonite education has deeply enriched his own life and that of many others. If you keep reading through the pages of this book, you'll be enriched as well.

> *Ervin R. Stutzman*
> *Executive Director,*
> *Mennonite Church USA*
> *Harrisonburg, Virginia*
> *October 2010*

Introduction

On January 8, 2002, President George W. Bush signed into law legislation aimed at transforming public education in the United States. The stated goals of the No Child Left Behind Act of 2001—to improve the performance of elementary and high school students by focusing on national standards—seemed uncontroversial. Nevertheless, in the years that followed, the legislation sparked a major public debate about education. For some, the new law finally made teachers and administrators accountable for the quality of education they were providing their students. Educators would no longer be permitted to turn a blind eye to high school illiteracy or the practice of social promotion. If underperforming schools did not implement dramatic reforms, they faced the prospect of state-mandated reorganization or loss of funding.

Others, however, sharply criticized the legislation. The reforms seemed to focus on a single measure of ability—test scores—as the standard of educational success or failure. At the same time, they imposed a uniform set of expectations that ignored fundamental differences in social, economic, and cultural contexts. Moreover, the federally mandated standards were often underfunded. As a result, art, music, and language courses disappeared, and dispirited teachers devoted more and more class time to test-taking strategies.

Regardless of your position on the legislation itself, the passionate public debate engendered by the No Child Left Behind Act made one thing very clear: education matters!

One concern driving the national debate over assessment, accountability, and measurable outcomes was simply the cold calculations of economic logic. In the fall of 2010 public school systems in the United States employed some 3.3 million elementary and secondary teachers to educate nearly 50 million students, with an additional 6 million students enrolled in private schools. In the 2010–2011 school year, U.S. taxpayers spent no less than $540 billion on elementary and secondary education alone, averaging nearly $10,800 per student. If we add to these figures the public investment in postsecondary education, the total outlay nearly doubles.[1] Clearly, our society is devoting a significant amount of national resources to the education of our children and young adults. Thus, when surveys suggest that math and literacy test scores, especially among U.S. students, are falling substantially behind their counterparts in other developed countries, people begin to ask: Is our national investment in education paying off? What are the consequences of a substandard education for the future well-being of our economy and nation?

Beyond the economic calculations, the debate over educational reforms is so passionate because we also recognize how closely education is linked to the well-being of individual lives. Personal success in our culture—whether defined as income, vocational choice, freedom of mobility, or even life-expectancy—is nearly inseparable from access to quality education. The debate matters because the education our children receive will likely set the trajectory of rest of their lives. The dreams, hopes, and aspirations of millions of young people hang in the balance.

But there are even deeper reasons for the emotional energy evident in the discussions. Since the beginning of human history, education—both formal and informal—has been the way societies have transmitted their deepest spiritual, cultural, and political values from one generation to the next. Unlike most other creatures, human babies enter the world completely immobile, with no teeth and no protective body hair. Instead of relying primarily on natural instincts, humans depend heavily on the transmission of cultural knowledge for their survival. Moreover, human adolescence extends for a long time during which youth are dependent on their families and the larger community. This means that human communities invest enormous social and economic resources in educating their young people, passing along not only the skills necessary for physical survival, but also the deeper knowledge, wisdom, and spiritual values that give life meaning and purpose.

Our first educational settings are always informal and come to us in the context of a family or local community. Almost immediately we are immersed in language, trusting those around us to speak slowly, simply, and clearly. Gradually, through exploration, play, and repetition, we develop motor skills and an awareness of cause-and-effect. In more subtle, but no less crucial, interactions with each other we begin to develop basic emotional and relational skills. As we mature, we become aware of the consequences of our choices, the mysteries of love and hate, the practices of faith and worship, and the larger spiritual realities that form the foundation of human dignity and meaningful moral decision making. Much of this happens without any conscious intentionality or design.

But education also happens more formally. Parents continually teach their children, often through repetition, how to function in complex social contexts by saying "please" and "thank you" or by shaking hands in formal greetings. We learn how to interact with the natural world around us by caring for pets, taking camping trips, and observing parental practices like recycling or gardening. Basic skills are passed from one generation to the next in kitchens, barns, and workshops, or as is more likely today, in classrooms, lecture halls, and laboratories.

At stake in all of these varied forms of education are fundamental assumptions about how the world works. Indeed, education is never *just* about literacy or preparation for a future job market. At its core, education is the means by which humans negotiate how they relate to each other, how they engage with the natural world, and how they understand ultimate questions of goodness, justice, and truth.

This is one reason so many parents and educators are troubled with defining educational outcomes by standardized tests—as seemed to be the case with the No Child Left Behind legislation. Lurking in the background of the current national discussion of educational methods and priorities are not just technical questions of teaching methods or delivery systems, but a host of value-laden concerns that go much deeper than demonstrated competence in a narrowly defined set of measurable outcomes. What, for example, is the relative role of public education compared with other social institutions like the family or church? How should the finite number of educational dollars be best apportioned? What is the nature of our commitment to children with special needs, to children who do not speak English as a first language, or to children who are hungry?

In answering these questions, we recognize a fact frequently hidden in the public debate. To the extent that our convictions about education inevitably rest on assumptions regarding things like truth, justice, and the nature of our commitments to each other, conversations about education are ultimately *religious* in nature. Our convictions about what should be passed along to the next generation—to what ends and by what pedagogical means—reveal our most basic assumptions about the world, our beliefs regarding human nature, our vision of the good society, and our understandings about how best to achieve that vision.

Every modern political system—whether it be contemporary variations of participatory democracy, the communism of Stalinist Russia, national socialism under Hitler, or the sharia law in Islamic countries—has given enormous attention to the nurture of children and young adults. Education is never a value-free enterprise, nor is it ever reducible only to competency in subjects like reading, writing, and arithmetic.

Education in a Mennonite Perspective

This book enters the larger public conversation on education by focusing on the religious foundations of teaching and learning as they have found expression in one particular Christian tradition: the Mennonites. Like all religious groups, Mennonites have a strong interest in communicating their distinctive beliefs and practices not only to their own members, but also to others who might be interested in their understanding of the Christian faith. From their beginnings in the Anabaptist movement of the sixteenth-century Reformation, groups in the Anabaptist-Mennonite tradition have passed along their faith in the form of stories, songs, confessions, and catechisms. For much of their history, Mennonites looked primarily to the home and congregation as the primary contexts for biblical teaching, for instruction in the formative rituals of prayer and worship, and for modeling Christian faith in daily life. But along the way

Mennonites have also been attentive to more formal structures of education as well.

Ever since their initial arrival in North America in 1683, Mennonites have cared about primary education, establishing some of the first schools in the Franconia and Lancaster regions of eastern Pennsylvania. These schools frequently met in congregational meetinghouses or in one-room structures built by members of the congregation. With the passage of the Pennsylvania Free Public School law in 1834, most of these schools became community schools, open to all area residents. For the next hundred years or so, Mennonites in the U.S. generally supported local public education—as taxpayers, parents, teachers and administrators—regarding it as an institution that served the common good.

During the twentieth century, North American Mennonites also became increasingly committed to providing an alternative to public education in the form of church-related private schools. Such schools—funded by private tuition dollars and organized around an explicitly faith-based mission—were created, like their public school counterparts, to provide basic academic instruction that would help children and young adults become productive citizens. But supporters of these church schools were also committed to nurturing students in Christian faith and practices, usually rooted quite consciously in the Anabaptist-Mennonite tradition.

By the opening decade of the twenty-first century, more than forty schools—ranging from prekindergarten to seminaries—were affiliated with Mennonite Education Agency (MEA), the organization charged by Mennonite Church USA with the responsibility of overseeing its program of church-related education.[2] On the whole, these schools are thriving today, blessed with gifted administrators, well-trained teachers, impressive facilities, strong academic traditions, and successful sports, arts, and music programs. At the same time, however, Mennonite education is in the midst of a significant religious, cultural, and economic transformation that poses some daunting and complex challenges for the future.

In its simplest form, those challenges may be summarized as follows:

1. All schools affiliated with MEA have chosen that relationship because they are committed, albeit with varying degrees of enthusiasm, to shaping their institutions around an understanding of the Christian faith informed by the Anabaptist-Mennonite tradition, a tradition that gives a distinctive focus to their identity. All the schools have framed their mission, pedagogy, and desired educational outcomes, implicitly at least, as an expression of this particular Christian tradition.

2. At the same time—and here is where tensions often emerge—the Anabaptist-Mennonite tradition in North America is itself in the midst of a profound transformation. For much of their history here, Mennonites have settled in relatively homogenous communities. In many of those communities, a strong congregational identity—sharpened by a view of the church as separated from the world, a commitment to pacifism that often set them at odds with their neighbors, and a general suspicion of worldly culture—fostered a sense of "otherness." This has persisted in subtle cultural forms long after Mennonites fully entered the modern world of professions, higher education, and cultural engagement. For a time, Mennonite identity could be distilled in a theological formulation, sometimes called "the Anabaptist vision." To be Mennonite meant that one identified with a distinctive theological tradition, rooted in the Radical Reformation of the sixteenth century, with a strong emphasis on discipleship, community, and an ethic of love.

By the end of the twentieth century, however, both the sociological and theological foundations of Mennonite identity were becoming increasingly tenuous. Like many mainline Protestant denominations in North America, Mennonite allegiance to denominational institutions has been steadily waning. Support for Mennonite publications, mission agencies, and service organizations, once simply assumed, now faces increasing competition from other groups. Despite an active mission outreach, Mennonite congregations are aging, and overall membership is static or slowly declining. Moreover, many Mennonites have become increasingly ambivalent about traditional theological distinctives such as pacifism or nonconformity to the dominant culture. Communal expressions of Christian life are outmoded. As a result, the various schools affiliated with MEA today, like their supporting congregations and conferences, reflect a range of theological orientations and cultural practices. What it means to be a "Mennonite school" or to embrace an "Anabaptist-Mennonite philosophy of education" is not entirely clear.

3. If this growing sense of internal diversity is a negative way of framing the context, a more positive perspective would be to highlight the renewed commitment to missional outreach evident in many Mennonite educational institutions. Although Mennonite schools were once largely a defensive means for preserving a sociological and theological birthright—with the overwhelming majority of students, teachers, and administrators rooted in local Mennonite congregations—today these schools embrace a broader mission. A growing number of students attending Mennonite schools have no direct connection to the Anabaptist-Mennonite tradition, yet they are attracted by features evident in these schools: the educational quality, the general religious ethos, the reputation for compassionate faculty, or the commitment to service,

international education, and peacemaking. Most Mennonite schools affirm this growing diversity in their student bodies, seeing it as a new opportunity for missional outreach. More than being simply a survival strategy in a competitive marketplace, nurturing relationships with people beyond the traditional boundaries of the Mennonite community remains a positive and consistent expression of the Anabaptist-Mennonite faith and one that has the potential to enliven and renew the tradition itself.

4. At the same time, this growing diversity inevitably raises a host of difficult and often-unarticulated questions that need to be addressed. What, for example, is the relationship between the identity of a school as a "Mennonite" institution and the growing diversity of the students being served by the school? What gives a school its distinctive Anabaptist-Mennonite character? How does an explicit association with MEA connect a school with the larger goals, identity, and vision of the Anabaptist-Mennonite tradition? How are those distinctive qualities communicated or embodied? If schools are to be truly missional in opening their classrooms to a much wider range of students, what form should the good news of God's reign take, and how might the success of that missional outreach be appropriately assessed? In its most basic form, how might Mennonite schools maintain a balance between the genuine hospitality of broad inclusion on the one hand and, on the other hand, a temptation to water down their distinctive identity in the interests of expanding enrollment or simply surviving?

In light of the growing diversity that has come to characterize Mennonite schools in recent decades—along with ongoing conversations within the Mennonite Church about questions of identity and the larger public debate over educational goals and assessment—MEA leaders have explored various ways to address these challenges. Among other initiatives, they have commissioned this book as a way of distilling some of the central features of an Anabaptist-Mennonite philosophy of education into an accessible format in the hopes that it might stimulate a broad and constructive conversation among congregations, parents, board members, and teachers.

What Is a Philosophy of Education?

To some ears, the phrase a "philosophy of education in an Anabaptist-Mennonite perspective" will sound dangerously abstract and theoretical. Although this book is not intended to provide a how-to guide on classroom management or engage the debate on best practices for teaching reading or math, I hope the chapters that follow will be practical, useful, and clear. Indeed, the book's central concern is to connect faith and practice—to link the world of Christian beliefs with the daily realities of the classroom.

The field of educational theory, of course, claims a long history of competing philosophies—including dozens of venerable names like John Dewey, Maria Montessori, Rudolf Steiner, and Paulo Friere—each grounded in a set of convictions about human nature, pedagogical methods, and ideal outcomes toward which education should be leading us. Texts devoted more specifically to philosophies of Christian education also abound. Some of these, especially those coming out of the Calvinist or Reformed tradition, emphasize rational argumentation and the development of a Christian worldview. Others, especially those favored by conservative evangelicals, focus on Christian doctrine and the most effective methods for inculcating orthodox theological convictions. Still others, reflecting the growing popularity of the homeschooling movement, offer an approach to education that aims to preserve a distinct way of life outside of the cultural mainstream and free from state control. All of these books constitute a rich and diverse literature that I will not try to systematically summarize or critique.[3]

When I use the phrase *philosophy of education*, I understand it to refer to the wonderfully complex pattern of relationships that join beliefs to practices, and to the conscious reflection about how these beliefs and practices are communicated and transformed in a school environment. In contrast to those in other Christian groups, educators in the Anabaptist-Mennonite tradition have traditionally not been very explicit or systematic about the educational philosophies that have guided their approach to education. Frequently Mennonites have simply borrowed—consciously or accidentally—from other traditions. Like much of Mennonite theology, the Mennonite philosophy of education has tended to be more implicit than explicit. Rather than consciously *expressed*, it has simply been *embodied*.[4]

Although there may be some wisdom behind this impulse, it is also clear that the Anabaptist-Mennonite tradition contains ample resources for articulating a distinctive philosophy of education. This book aims to make more explicit what now is implicit behind the practices of Mennonite education—how we teach, what we teach, the overarching goals of our classrooms, the way we think about teaching and learning—all in the hopes that this exploration will stimulate more discussion among board members, administrators, teachers, parents, and pastors about the value of Mennonite education.

A philosophy of education in an Anabaptist-Mennonite perspective, as I suggest in what follows, consists of three interrelated themes.

1. *Theological emphases common to all Mennonite educational institutions*

A philosophy of education distinctly Anabaptist-Mennonite in character must begin with some shared understandings about theology. Defining these will not be a straightforward or simple matter. As a rule, Mennonites have not anchored their identity in highly centralized structures of church authority or in a checklist of orthodox doctrines. Yet despite some inevitable nuance in emphases, schools affiliated with MEA align themselves with a theology anchored in an *incarnational* or Christocentric understanding of the gospel, which calls for a strong emphasis on God's revelation to the world in the life, teachings, death, and resurrection of Jesus Christ. This implies that Mennonite schools will be shaped by a Christ-centered way of reading Scripture, a Christ-centered understanding of relationships with other people, and a Christ-centered view of the church as the visible form of the resurrected Jesus in the world today.

Because theological identity is always a dynamic matter, describing Mennonite theology in terms of the incarnation is the beginning, not the end, of the conversation. Indeed, one characteristic of an incarnational approach is the recognition that faith always finds expression in particular contexts and in distinctive forms that vary from place to place. But for all the healthy variety evident among Mennonite schools today, there should still be an identifiable cluster of emphases as well as a shared framework of convictions that bring these local differences into a larger coherence. One goal of this book is to offer a language for those distinctive themes, not with the intention of drawing sharp boundaries, but to strengthen a clearer sense of purpose behind the educational goals of all Mennonite-related schools.

2. A pedagogy informed by Anabaptist-Mennonite convictions

To have any integrity, theological convictions always find expression in visible habits and practices. In the educational setting, the primary focus of our shared practice is teaching, along with the web of relationships that form around the learning process. The art of teaching, sometimes called *pedagogy*, draws on a complex mix of classroom environment, assumptions about learning, student-teacher relationships, expertise regarding content, and a larger awareness of purpose and goals.

As in the case of Anabaptist-Mennonite theology, we assume that pedagogy in Mennonite schools is expressed in more than one way—after all, classroom settings range from preschool to graduate programs, and teachers will vary in personality and style. Such differences can be honored and even embraced. But a pedagogy shaped in the Anabaptist-Mennonite tradition by a theology of incarnation should reflect a shared ethos and a distinctive set of dispositions or attitudes that will be evident to visitors to any Mennonite classroom or school. Among other things, for example, all teachers at Mennonite institutions will model dispositions like curiosity, joy, patience, and love. And those dispositions will unfold within a larger set of shared practices—what I call the "invisible curriculum"—that create an environment within which education in an Anabaptist-Mennonite mode can flourish.

3. Outcomes that reflect Anabaptist-Mennonite distinctives

Finally, a philosophy of education in an Anabaptist-Mennonite perspective should encourage schools to embrace a common identity in terms of educational goals or outcomes. Woven into the theological convictions and pedagogical assumptions of Mennonite schools is an overarching sense of purpose and direction, often identified as the *mission* of the school. Here too, we can expect to find variety. The mission statements of various Mennonite educational institutions reflect a range of emphases, depending on local settings and contexts. But defining an overarching set of shared outcomes encourages Mennonite schools to think more intentionally about their theology and pedagogy and to engage more confidently in the shared enterprise of Christian education. This book will be bold in identifying several ideal outcomes of education in Mennonite schools, framed in the context of an incarnational theology and a set of embodied practices.

In short, this book seeks to join a *rationale* for Mennonite education (the *why* that inevitably raises questions of theology) with the distinctive *practices* that one might expect to find in all Mennonite classrooms (the *how* themes of pedagogy). Together the rationale and practices shape the *content* of Mennonite education (the *what* of the learning outcomes).

Challenges and Limitations of This Book

I gladly accepted the invitation to write this book. After all, my wife and I were deeply shaped by our experiences as students at a Mennonite high school and college. In addition, I have spent twenty-five years teaching at a Mennonite college, and our four children have repeated our experience of attending a Mennonite secondary school and college. We are profoundly grateful for the ways that Mennonite educators have shaped our family's life. Moreover, I accepted the challenge of writing this book because I am convinced that healthy and vibrant Mennonite educational programs are essential for a renewal of the Anabaptist-Mennonite witness in our communities and world. I believe strongly that the Anabaptist-Mennonite tradition has a distinctive gift to offer the world within God's wider purposes, and I am eager to share the insights and convictions that I have gleaned from my journey within that tradition.

Yet I also recognize that the challenges of writing a philosophy of education in an Anabaptist-Mennonite perspective are daunting. In a spirit of transparency, it may be helpful to acknowledge several limitations of this project right from the start.

1. The broad scope of this book is intended to cover educational settings from prekindergarten schools to elementary and secondary schools as well as colleges/ universities and seminaries. Each of these schools has emerged in a distinctive geographical setting, including the urban contexts of Philadelphia and Pasadena; the rich farm country of Ohio, Indiana, Iowa, and Pennsylvania; the plains of Kansas and South Dakota; and extending beyond the continental United States to Canada and the island of Puerto Rico. Each of these schools has its own unique history and identity, along with its own governance structure, networks of support, and niche in the local community. Some schools are clearly intent on preserving and promoting Anabaptist-Mennonite distinctives; others look on their Mennonite ties as a burden or even an embarrassment. Inevitably this institutional context will shape the assumptions that readers bring to the themes presented here, thus making some aspects of the book seem irrelevant or misguided.

2. Behind these differences in history, governance, and mission lie deeper realities of the theological diversity gathered under the Mennonite umbrella. Given this diversity, it is presumptuous for an author to speak on behalf of the church or to pretend that the theological perspective sketched here is a fixed baseline of Mennonite orthodoxy. My goal is to provide a framework—rooted in the biblical story, true to the distinctive themes of the Anabaptist-

Mennonite tradition, and informed by a living, dynamic Christian faith—but not to provide the definitive or final word. Nevertheless, even though the schools affiliated with Mennonite Education Agency will likely not be in complete unity about every aspect of Mennonite faith and practice, I hope that they can agree that a common conversation, shaped by the contours of the Anabaptist-Mennonite tradition, is possible and worthwhile.

3. I realize that education happens in many different settings: in our homes and congregations, in our interaction with neighbors in the community, in our professional involvements, and perhaps even more profoundly, in the many hours spent with TV, movies, the Internet, and other media. In a book focused on church-related education, it is easy to assume that formal education in classroom settings is the primary, maybe even the only, context in which Christian formation occurs. Yet this is emphatically not the case. To be sure, children do spend many more waking hours at school than they do at home. We know that teachers are often extremely important role models for young people. Child psychologists agree that peer groups play a significant role in shaping adolescent values. Still, schools are not the only variable in shaping Christian identity. Many young Christians have grown into mature Christians without ever attending a church-related school. Conversely, not all students attending a Mennonite school emerge with a deep or enduring commitment to Christ. So even though this book is focused on Christian education and seeks to make a compelling argument in favor of Anabaptist-Mennonite schools, I do not believe that this is the *only* path that will lead to mature faith, strong churches, or vibrant witness.

4. Finally, because this book is intended for a broad audience, parts will connect more immediately with some readers than with others. For those already committed to Mennonite education, I hope that the book will not only

restate the obvious, but also open new territory with a fresh focus and rationale. I trust that veteran teachers, administrators, and boards will recognize the philosophical and pedagogical themes addressed here. But I also anticipate that those same themes will help to orient new teachers, board members, and principals to the landscape they are entering. In a similar way, the theological themes sketched in the book will likely be familiar to longtime, convinced members of the Mennonite church, but I trust that the ideas will also be accessible to newcomers to the Mennonite church.

Most of all, I hope that my description of Christian pedagogy in an Anabaptist-Mennonite perspective will interest all those who care about sustaining and renewing the faith practices and convictions that have sustained the Anabaptist-Mennonite family of faith for nearly five centuries, whether they are longtime supporters of Mennonite education or skeptics and critics of our church schools.

An Overview of What Follows

The outline of the book is quite simple. Chapter 1 sketches a history of education within the Western tradition. It details the emergence of Mennonite schools in North America during the course of the twentieth century and the more recent transformation in Mennonite education, moving from a focus primarily on the children of Mennonite families to a broader outreach intended for a diverse student body. Later chapters describe the consequences of this shift for future Mennonite education, particularly in terms of theological identity, pedagogical approaches, and anticipated outcomes.

Chapter 2 develops a theological foundation for Christian education, focusing primarily on the incarnation. In the Anabaptist-Mennonite tradition, being a Christian has less to do with abstract beliefs or doctrinal claims than with the relationships that follow from a conviction that God is revealed most fully to human beings in the life, teachings, death, and resurrection of Jesus Christ. In Jesus, we see God—the Word made flesh. Being a follower of Jesus is not simply a personal reality ("having Jesus in my heart"). It is also a commitment to participate with other Christians in the radical possibility that Christ's kingdom is indeed coming "on earth as it is in heaven" (Matt 6:10). The rest of the book is an extended reflection on what a theology of the incarnation might mean in an educational context.

Chapter 3 describes the outlines of an Anabaptist-Mennonite pedagogy. We look first at the "invisible curriculum," or the ethos, of the school and then at the practices we might expect to find in teachers who are committed to seeing God's presence in creation and bearing witness to God's ongoing revelation in the world. An Anabaptist-Mennonite pedagogy will be attentive to practices that point to God's intentions for humanity in our relationship with God, creation, and each other.

Chapter 4 addresses the question of goals or outcomes—a familiar theme to educators. What is the *telos* or the "end" to which an education in an Anabaptist-Mennonite context should be directed? What shared expectations about work do teachers and administrators hold for which they are willing to be held accountable? In short, what is the added value that parents and congregations might legitimately assume is part of an education at a Mennonite school?

Clearly not everyone will agree with the ideas proposed in these chapters. But this is as it should be: Vigorous debate enlivens and renews healthy schools. Chapter 5 encourages this exchange by identifying some tough questions that emerge in conversations about Mennonite education and offering a succinct but frank response. The questions identified here are not exhaustive, and readers may find the responses frustratingly brief or even wrong. But my goal in chapter 5 is to encourage a spirit of openness and transparency: No question regarding Mennonite education should be off-limits even if you do not find the response offered here fully convincing.

I conclude with a brief final chapter to reorient the discussion on Mennonite education beyond the past and present and toward the future. The field of education is notoriously susceptible to shiny new models, paradigms, strategies, and techniques. At the same time, educational institutions, especially colleges and universities, are equally notorious for their resistance to change. So chapter 6, an opening exercise in eschatological thinking, imagines an alternative future shaped by a keen sense of the Spirit's capacity to "make all things new" (Rev 21:5). How might Mennonite educators be clear-sighted about current realities even as they live with anticipation into expressions of God's kingdom yet to come?

Taste and See

One Sunday morning in a young adult Sunday school class that I have taught for many years, a young man about to graduate from college was reflecting on a similar moment in his life some four or five years earlier. During his final semester of high school, a beloved teacher at the Mennonite school he attended announced a diversion from the normal routine. Instead of meeting in their classroom, he had students put on their winter garb and followed him through the snow to a nearby cemetery. For the next hour, the teacher led his students on a meandering tour, stopping at various gravestones to offer some memories—a story, a brief biography, a testimony—of various deceased members of the community who had been part of the school and had shaped his life. "These are the people who helped to form me as a human being—a brother, a father, a teacher, a Christian," the elderly teacher said. "They have left a legacy to me and to this school. And now it's time to pass that legacy along to you as well."

Then, in the stark beauty of the cold cemetery, he turned to his students, all of them eager to move on to the next stage of their lives, and asked: "What will be your calling? What will you do with the gifts that have been entrusted to you? What will be your legacy?"

As the young man recounted that memory to the rest of the Sunday school class, while anticipating his impending graduation from college and another new chapter of life, he broke down and wept.

What is the appropriate measure of an education? What is it that *really* matters? What does it mean to encounter God and to be transformed by that encounter? The psalmists wrestle with that question in almost every verse of that wonderful book. Indeed, throughout the Psalms we glimpse into the inner world of a student's struggle for clarity in the classroom of life. For the writers of the Psalms, God is never an abstraction—a list of beliefs, a set of doctrines, or a compilation of truth claims. Instead, God is always encountered in the dynamic mystery of relationships. And those relationships potentially include *all* of creation: rocks, meadows, mountains, thunder, rain. The God of the psalmists is both fearsomely awe-inspiring and compassionate, a mighty warrior and a gentle shepherd, creator of the heavens and earth as well as the one who knit us in our mother's womb and knew us before we were born.

On the day that I agreed to write this book, the lectionary reading included this familiar passage from Psalm 34.

> Taste and see that the LORD is good;
> blessed is the [one] who takes refuge in him.
> Fear the LORD, you his saints,
> for those who fear him lack nothing.
> The lions may grow weak and hungry,
> but those who seek the LORD lack no good thing.
> Come, my children, listen to me;
> I will teach you the fear of the LORD.
> Whoever of you loves life
> and desires to see many good days,
> keep your tongue from evil
> and your lips from speaking lies.
> Turn from evil and do good;
> seek peace and pursue it.
>   —Psalm 34:8-14

The psalmist's words in these simple yet wondrously complex musings have inspired me in the months since. And I think this same passage must also have informed the pedagogical perspective of the teacher who led his students on a wintry tour of the cemetery. At the heart of a Christian education, this psalmist suggests, is "the fear of the LORD" (v. 11). This is not the cowering fear of a victim, but a joyful posture of worship that recognizes our rightful place as creatures in a world that God has created and continues to sustain. "Fear of the LORD" also suggests that we are mindful of our mortality—that we live our lives within the horizon of eternity. Those who have learned to "fear the LORD," the psalmist continues, will be attentive to their speech ("Keep your tongue from evil and your lips from speaking lies") and committed to reconciled relationships with others ("Turn from evil and do good; seek peace and pursue it"). Those who take refuge in the Lord are numbered as "saints" and will "lack no good thing."

But all this begins with a God encounter rooted in our physical senses and in the goodness of creation itself: "Taste and see," the psalmist writes, "Taste and see that the LORD is good."

In the end, this book is less an argument about a philosophy of education in an Anabaptist-Mennonite perspective, than it is an invitation to encounter God through the gift of the "Word made flesh" (John 1:14). Together let us reflect on how the legacy entrusted to us might be offered as a gift to others.

Taste and see that the Lord is good!

The Context of Mennonite Education in North America

You could almost say that the Mennonite school at Greenwood, Delaware, began by accident. For more than a century, Mennonite families had been moving into the Casselman River area of western Maryland, attracted by the rich farmland and ready access to markets. In the early 1900s, a group of settlers moved eastward and began to buy up farms across the state line in Delaware. In 1914 they officially organized as the Greenwood Mennonite Church. Although their dress, language, and worship style set them apart from the larger community, Mennonites in Greenwood lived in peace with their Lutheran, Reformed, and Catholic neighbors. Their children studied and played together in the local public schools, and the Mennonites and their neighbors interacted with each other in agricultural life and business dealings.

But in the uneasy years after the conclusion of World War I, many Americans began to express new anxieties over the nation's role in the world. Concerns about the rising number of immigrants and debates about national identity and the role of the League of Nations prompted some groups to promote greater public awareness of the national Pledge of Allegiance. Some even insisted that the pledge be required as a daily practice in the nation's public schools as a way of inculcating the virtues of citizenship and deepening a sense of national pride. On April

15, 1925, the state legislature of Delaware introduced a law requiring that the American flag be displayed in every school classroom. The law also mandated that all school-age children "salute and pledge allegiance" to the flag each morning.[5]

Although some families in the Greenwood Mennonite community were indifferent to the idea of their children's pledging allegiance, others had serious reservations. For them, the pledge was a formative ritual, dangerously close to an act of idolatry and clearly intended to inculcate a spirit of nationalism in their children. With memories of a world war fresh in mind, pledging allegiance to the nation implied a readiness to bear arms in defense of the country—a clear violation of the Mennonite commitment to nonresistance and their conviction that allegiance to Christ should come before the call of the nation.

After a flurry of conversations with denominational leaders, state politicians, and representatives of the local school board, the Mennonite congregation of Greenwood decided that their children would not participate in the daily ritual. For several years classroom teachers did not protest when the Mennonite children in their classes remained seated during the Pledge of Allegiance. But early in 1928 a school board member lodged a vigorous public complaint to the state's superintendent of public instruction. Abstaining from the pledge, he insisted, was a clear violation of the law. In response, the superintendent demanded that the principal enforce the requirement and threatened legal action if Mennonite students failed to comply.

More than eighty years later, David Yoder, then a fourth grader at Greenwood Elementary, could vividly remember what happened next. "The principal, Miss Gibson, took all the Mennonite children to the basement and told us to pledge allegiance. I remember crying, but we still didn't say the pledge. So she sent us home and said we could not return until we agreed to participate."[6]

Thus was born Greenwood Mennonite School. Without a great deal of planning or fanfare, the Mennonite congregation in Greenwood simply created an alternative school. Initially, the children gathered in the church's meetinghouse, where they sat on benches and received instruction from the pastor, Nevin Bender. With nearly thirty students enrolled the following fall, the school organized more formally, adding grade-level textbooks, a chalkboard, and actual school desks. By 1932 families pooled their resources to build a schoolhouse of their own.

The Greenwood school was not the first time Mennonites in North America ventured into the world of church-related education. Like most other religious groups who settled in colonial Pennsylvania, Mennonites often sent their children to small schools that operated out of their meetinghouses or in small structures constructed by the congregation. Christopher Dock (ca. 1698–1771), a Mennonite schoolteacher from Skippack and widely acknowledged to be one of the foremost educational theorists of his day, taught at such a school. Following the passage of the Free School Law in 1834, Pennsylvania Mennonites generally complied with the new state regulations establishing mandatory public education and sent their children to the newly created rural public schools. In the new context, they continued to be heavily involved as teachers and school directors.[7]

In 1868, the General Conference Mennonite Church created a short-lived seminary in Wadsworth, Ohio. During the decades that followed, Mennonites elsewhere in the United States went on to establish no fewer than six colleges or academies. But the Greenwood Mennonite School of 1928 marked the beginning of an energetic flurry of new interest in church-related education. During the next twenty-five years, scores of articles on Christian education appeared in denominational periodicals. By the beginning of the twenty-first century, groups affiliated with the General Conference Mennonite Church and the Mennonite Church had created more than forty schools, covering the full educational spectrum from early childhood to seminary.

At the same time, however, Mennonites were by no means unanimous in their enthusiasm for church-based alternatives to public education. Many Mennonites, like most Americans, regarded state-sponsored public education to be as self-evident as public utilities or functioning highways. The home and congregation were the appropriate settings for religious instruction; tax-paying members of a pluralistic society, they assumed, should support public schools. After all, the argument ran, modern democracies can survive only if the electorate is literate and only if education is equally accessible to all citizens, regardless of economic status, race, or religion. For many members of Anabaptist-Mennonite congregations, these arguments seemed self-evident. There was no good reason to create a church-based alternative to the public school system.

Yet considered within the broad sweep of the Western tradition, it is actually state-sponsored public education that is the more recent innovation. For most of Western history, education properly understood was the prerogative of the church. The story of how the state came to claim responsibility for public education—effectively wresting it away from church control—suggests that the twentieth-century Mennonite impulse to return to church-based education has a deep historical precedent, ultimately going all the way back to the Jewish torah schools of Old Testament times. Understanding this context puts the current debate over church-related education within a much broader perspective.

The Transformation of Public Education in the Modern West

The transformation of formal education in the West from an institution controlled by the church—structured around the study of theology and infused with a certainty that all true knowledge revealed the presence of God in creation—into the secular model of public education that we know today is a complex story, far more complex than this simple summary might suggest. Nonetheless, the basic outlines of that transformation can be described in terms of five major, related shifts that establish the context for the emergence and flourishing of Mennonite schools in North America during the course of the twentieth century.

From Church Control to State Control: The Secularization of Education

One of the first steps in the birth of modern public education was a fundamental shift in the control of educational institutions from the church to the state, and, in a parallel fashion, a shift away from theology as the focal point of education to a curriculum in which theology became one field of study among many. That transformation was slow and uneven, but its consequences have been dramatic, especially in college or university settings.

What we think of as modern universities today are the heirs of a much longer tradition with roots going back to Catholic monastic and cathedral schools of the Middle Ages. Following the collapse of the Roman Empire in the fourth and fifth centuries, new centers of knowledge began to emerge within the Catholic church as local bishops established schools, usually associated with their cathedrals, that educated future clergy in the basic skills of reading and writing. Gradually a formal curriculum emerged—centered on seven *liberal arts*—that became the foundation for many of the disciplines of university study still common today.

Over time, some of these schools began to accept children of the wealthy nobility. And eventually many students in medieval universities were trained for secular careers as court officials, lawyers, or civic bureaucrats. Nevertheless, the curriculum of the medieval schools was overwhelmingly religious in nature. Theology was clearly the "queen of the sciences," and *all* knowledge—math, music, rhetoric, and grammar—was understood to be an expression of God's revelation. In this sense, there was no significant distinction between secular and religious education. Education was always understood to be in the service of faith and an act of worship to God. "Love of knowledge and desire for God" were the famous words of the Italian theologian Thomas Aquinas. When Aquinas died in 1274, he was still working on his *Summa theologica*, a vast compendium of knowledge that traces the interconnectedness of all creation from the inanimate base elements of the earth, through humans and angels, all the way to the Creator. In the Catholic tradition, the study of nature was inextricably fused with the revelation of God. Reason, properly applied, would always lead the faithful inquirer to a deeper understanding of God's presence in the created world.

With the Renaissance and the Protestant Reformation, however, this fusion of faith and knowledge began to slowly unravel. Renaissance thinkers began to describe the world in terms that were quantifiable and measurable, paying careful attention to the demonstrable principles of cause-and-effect as explanations for natural phenomena. The reformer Martin Luther insisted on an absolute distinction between the inner world of the Christian life (where God's gift of grace was freely bestowed) and the external world of rituals, practices, and deeds (which he associated with "works righteousness"). Although neither the Renaissance humanists nor the Protestant Reformers intended these distinctions to lead to a sharp division between the sacred and the secular, their thought encouraged a broader trend toward separating the world of *faith* (thought to be subjective, private, and ultimately beyond the scope of reason) from the world of *science* (thought to be objective, public, and rational).

As modern nation-states gained increasing authority over the church, competing commitments to religious orthodoxy, especially during the so-called Wars of Religion in the seventeenth century, seemed to be the source of endless violence and social disorder. Eventually, in what we today call the "modern" world, scientific reason—with its claim to transcend religion, superstition, and ignorance—became the common coin of the realm. The new secular state was expected to be religiously neutral. It was supposed to tolerate all religions but only on the condition that believers kept religious claims out of the public arena and refrained from imposing their particular religious beliefs—which the state regarded as personal, private, and subjective—on anyone else.

The nineteenth century witnessed the emergence of the German model of a research university, in which scholars asserted a fundamental distinction between *facts*—which could be measured, tested, and independently verified—and *values*, which were subjective, culturally conditioned beliefs that could not be tested by experimentation or proofs. In place of theology, which had once permeated all subject areas of the medieval university, new fields of study emerged—the so-called *social sciences*—that promised to bring the rational logic and empirical research methods of science to the study of human behavior. Thus were created a host of new disciplines such as psychology (the scientific study of the mind), sociology (the scientific study of societies), anthropology (the scientific study of culture), economics (the scientific study of the market), and political science (the scientific study of politics). Theology itself was superseded by the newly created discipline of *religious studies*, which promised to bring a value-neutral, objective approach to the study of all world religions without privileging Christianity.

In this new educational order, religious convictions were understood to be private matters—appropriate for personal devotions or Sunday morning worship, but not as a focus of serious academic study. Instead, each denomination created parallel, privately funded educational institutions, called seminaries, in which they were free to train ministers and promote their own doctrinal orthodoxies in whatever manner they wished.

Most Americans today would agree in principle with the separation of church and state; and they would likely affirm the dominant role of the state in public education. At the same time, however, lingering uncertainties remain in our culture about the appropriate place of religion in the public square. For example, the various medieval Saints Days, once celebrated in public by all Catholic Christians, are now gone, but Americans are far less clear about relinquishing the public celebration of other religious holidays such as Christmas and Easter (whose observances are still marked in the public school calendar). Few would advocate for a state-sponsored religion, but many Americans continue to be deeply conflicted about the appropriateness of prayer before graduation ceremonies or whether schools should teach creationism in science classes, include Christmas carols in their music programs, or grant club status to campus Bible study groups.

In general, U.S. courts have ruled in favor of the secular character of public schools. Because a free and democratic society is committed to equality under the law, our public schools must, in principle, be as welcoming to Buddhists, Muslims, Baha'is, Jews, or students of no faith at all, as they are to Christians. Yet many Christians continue to chafe at these restrictions, secretly wishing that the state would offer more visible support for their religious convictions, especially in public education.

Whatever your opinion on these matters, the long-term transformation is clear. Although education was once regarded as the task of the church, with theology as the "queen of the sciences," today that role has been claimed by the state, which presides over an explicitly secular curriculum.

Democratization of Access to Education

Closely related to the secularization of education was a parallel shift in educational access. For most of human history, the great majority of people have spent virtually all of their waking hours in farming, struggling each season to raise enough food to feed themselves with a bit of seed corn remaining to plant the following year. The idea of taking young people out of the labor force, precisely at the time when they were best able to contribute to the household economy, was an unthinkable luxury. Thus, until fairly recently, formal classroom instruction in the Western tradition was restricted to the political or religious elite. The young people of Athens who gathered for conversation with Socrates and Plato were, for the most part, children of wealthy families, with plenty of free time on their hands to debate and philosophize. The first students of the monastic and cathedral schools, along with the early universities in Europe, all came from privileged classes and were trained to occupy positions of ecclesial or political authority.

All of this changed rather dramatically following the eighteenth-century political revolutions in France and the United States. With the birth of modern democracies came the new phenomenon of *mass* education. If democratic governance were truly to be a thing "of the people," the logic ran, then the nation's citizenry needed to be educated in the *liberal arts*, meaning the arts that are necessary for a free (from Latin, *liber*) people to rule itself. Responsible self-governance requires training in literacy, numeracy, historical perspectives, and critical thinking. Thus was born the modern tradition of publicly funded education accessible to all members of society, regardless of social status or economic means.

Not only was this new model of education to be accessible to everyone, it also was *obligatory*. Now, for the first time, legislators passed laws making it mandatory for all children to attend school, at least through the eighth grade; and truancy officers were appointed to enforce these laws. Parents who failed to send their children to school faced the likelihood of legal action including, in some cases, fines and imprisonment.

In the United States this same democratizing impulse has extended beyond elementary and high school to include college. In the course of the twentieth century, the creation of land-grant universities, community colleges, and state universities has made advanced education accessible and affordable to virtually all members of society. Today nearly 70 percent of all high school graduates enroll in college the following fall. In 2010 some 19.1 million students enrolled in U.S. public colleges and universities, with another 4.6 million studying at private institutions. The twentieth century also witnessed a dramatic rise in the number of women in higher education, so that today nearly 60 percent of all college students are women. All told, some 41 percent of eighteen to twenty-four year olds in the United States are enrolled in college.[8]

Citizenship and Comportment: Education in National Identity

Why, one might ask, would a state compel all of its citizens to attend school? One reason, as we have already noted, is to ensure that its citizens have the basic skills necessary for self-governance. An even deeper concern in modern democracies is for all citizens to be united by a common commitment to the nation and its ideals. Universal, mandatory education is the best way to achieve that goal. As the modern state claimed greater control over public education, it was inevitable that both the organization of educational institutions and the content of its curriculum would reflect the changing needs and interests of the state.

In a manner analogous to the role of theology in the medieval university, state-sponsored education also has a unifying focus at the very center of its curriculum: to educate young people in the deepest values and assumptions of the nation—what might be called the modern religion of citizenship. No longer is theology the glue that holds all of society together. Instead, modern democracies today are united by the common patriotism of their citizens. In the twenty-first century, most—though not all—modern people look back on the religious wars of the seventeenth century as a repulsive and ignorant form of religious zealotry. Yet at the same time most Americans do not think it at all odd that the state should ask them to kill in defense of political convictions or ideological commitments.

In the modern world, public schools are the settings for training children in the stories, ideals, virtues, and heroism of the nation, thereby ensuring that national identity passes along intact from one generation to the next. In schools, young people are inculcated in the principles of citizenship, formed by such rituals as saying the Pledge of Allegiance, singing the national anthem, posting flags in classrooms, holding public assemblies to honor war heroes, and commemorating patriotic festivals—all reasonable activities in public schools for basic training in the virtues of democracy, patriotism, and citizenship.

Some readers may be uncomfortable with this characterization of public education: the primary focus of schools, you might insist, is to help children become literate, not to train them to become warriors. Fair enough. My point here is not to suggest that public education is evil or devoted single-mindedly to the cause of nationalism. But we should also be absolutely clear that state-sponsored education is *not value neutral*. Ultimately a nation-state survives by the willingness of its citizens to kill and to die in its defense, and public schools are the primary settings in which young people learn the virtues of citizenship.

Professionalization of Education

At the beginning of the twentieth century, the most common form of elementary education in the United States was one- or two-room country schools, scattered across the rural landscape and governed by a locally elected school board. The teachers of these schools often had minimal training. They were poorly paid, the turnover rate was high, and educational standards varied widely from school to school.

Much of this changed in the first half of the twentieth century. Drawing on an expanding tax base and new legislative mandates, counties and local municipalities across the nation began to shut down one-room schools in order to consolidate them into larger regional schools with sparkling facilities, an expanded curriculum, a new focus on athletics, and the promise of an education oriented to the future rather than the past.

Accompanying these reforms were other innovations that brought a higher level of scientific rigor and professional standards to the field of education. Many state legislatures, for example, enacted new requirements regarding the training and certification of teachers. Accrediting organizations emerged to bring uniform standards to various programs of study. A new growth industry of educational

consultants flourished, each promoting an innovative pedagogy of reading or math and eager to sell vast numbers of
textbooks to accompany their system. Universities began
to offer advanced degrees in educational theory and school
administration. And teachers organized themselves into
unions, creating a powerful political force to promote their
professional interests through collective bargaining.

In the first half of the twentieth century, all these initiatives, and many others, were part of a larger movement
toward the scientific management of society. The current
fascination with standardized testing, new educational
delivery systems driven by advanced technology, and competing proposals for how to save "failing schools" are only
the most recent expressions of a long series of attempts to
legitimate the field of education as a true academic discipline, subject to the same research methodologies and professional standards as any other social science.

Expansion of Mandate

Finally, alongside the growing specialization and professionalization of American public education has been a
steady expansion in the scope of its mandate. Though the
basic goals of rural schools were quite specific—to promote the three R's of "reading, 'riting, and 'rithmetic"—
today we look to the public school system to serve a wide
range of functions that go far beyond education, narrowly
defined. As the number of households with two working
parents continues to rise, along with the average number
of hours that young people spend watching TV, school-
aged young people are reading far less at home than they
once did. Schools providing instruction in the basics of
reading often do so in the near absence of pleasure reading that used to happen at home. Or to cite a different
kind of example, first- and second-grade teachers report
spending more classroom time instructing children in basic

relational skills—helping them learn to say "please" and "thank you," practice the discipline of taking turns, or respond empathetically to the pain of others.

Meanwhile, guidance counselors are struggling to keep up with a growing range of psychological needs, rising incidences of attention-deficit/hyperactivity disorder (ADHD), and heightened concerns about bullying or school violence. School nurses are often overwhelmed with the challenge of tracking the many medications that students are taking while also tending to their basic health needs. A full range of specialists has emerged to address the unique challenges of children with physical, mental, or emotional disabilities. Today special education teachers, reading specialists, pedagogy coaches, and experts in teaching English to children of recent immigrants are all part of a standard staff at most elementary schools.

Many of these new public school functions have emerged without a great deal of public debate or discussion. Now understood to be essential elements of public school life, they also raise new questions about what, exactly, we expect from the educational system.

Although this brief history is far too simple, it highlights aspects of modern public education that many Americans assume are inevitable or simply part of the natural order of things. Modern public education is a secular enterprise, properly run by the state. It is not only accessible to everyone, but also mandatory. Beyond basic literacy or numeracy, public education instills the virtues of patriotism. Its culture mirrors the scientific logic and professional organization of other academic disciplines. And it has a very expansive mandate, which now includes a wide range of basic social services once assumed to be the responsibility of the family and local community.

All of these developments are relevant for understanding the emergence of Mennonite church-based alternatives to public education during the course of the twentieth century. It is to that story that we now turn.

Alternatives to Public Education

The Origins of Mennonite Education in North America

Even as public education was becoming a deeply entrenched assumption of modern life, with wide-ranging implications for almost every aspect of American society, alternative educational options have always existed alongside the dominant trend. Private preparatory schools, for example, building on an older European tradition of elite education, provided children of wealthy families with a useful setting for socializing with their upper-class peers, as well as an inside track to prize jobs or entrance into the nation's most elite universities. In a similar vein, families eager to expose their children to the discipline associated with military training or hoping to advance their prospects of a career in the armed forces, have long had the option of sending their children to military schools.

However, the strongest alternatives to public education have always been found within religious communities, especially among groups with a distinctive theological, cultural, or ethical identity that they hope to pass along to the next generation. In the United States, for example, the Jewish and Catholic faiths have long provided educational options for their young people that offer explicit training in the language, texts, theology, and rituals of their religious traditions. During the twentieth century the Reformed tradition has also aggressively promoted church-related alternatives to public education. In more recent years conservative

Christian groups have created hundreds of private schools and homeschooling associations, usually nondenominational in a formal sense, but clearly united by a commitment to inculcating a specific set of doctrinal convictions and a faith-infused perspective in all areas of study.

As a group, Mennonites are relative newcomers to the conversation about church-based education. Part of this can be explained by a long history of skepticism toward formal education in general. During the early years of the Reformation, many Anabaptist leaders were university-trained scholars, fluent in Latin, Greek, and even Hebrew. As they engaged in debates with Catholic theologians and the Protestant Reformers, however, they became increasingly suspicious about the relationship between university education and Christian faithfulness—specifically, the apparent gap between theory and practice. In their minds, it was precisely the learned doctors of the church (*Schriftgelehrten,* in German) who resorted to sophisticated and needlessly complicated arguments as a strategy to avoid the plain and simple teachings of Jesus.

When this first generation of university-educated Anabaptist leaders passed from the scene—often as martyrs—people of humbler status assumed leadership of the movement. Forced to flee from urban areas, Anabaptists in Switzerland and South Germany sought refuge in remote regions, where they could practice their faith in relative peace. There, cut off from formal paths to education, later generations of Anabaptists focused on agrarian skills. They were content if their children achieved a basic level of literacy sufficient to read Scripture, study the catechism, and sing from the hymnal. Over time the Mennonite and Amish descendants of these Anabaptists adopted a peasant skepticism about the utility of formal education. "The more learned, the more confused" (in German, *je gelehrte, je verkehrte*) was a common saying.

By contrast, Anabaptist groups in the Netherlands,

northern Germany, and eventually South Russia were far more positive about the merits of formal education. Although officially excluded from theological studies, Dutch Anabaptists attended the universities of their day, and they earned advanced degrees in a variety of disciplines with a strong concentration in engineering and medicine. By the eighteenth century Mennonites in the Netherlands were participating fully in all aspects of Dutch culture. As they became wealthy, their enthusiasm for education increased, often in the form of scholarships for young students, the creation of private libraries, or prizes for research and publications in a wide range of fields. Already in 1711 Mennonites in the Netherlands established a seminary in Amsterdam. Throughout the eighteenth and nineteenth centuries, they vigorously engaged the theological debates of their day, publishing hundreds of books, pamphlets, broadsides, hymnals, and confessions of faith.

Conditions were somewhat more restrictive in the Vistula Delta region of Poland/Prussia, where Mennonite communities also flourished in the seventeenth and eighteenth centuries. But in the early nineteenth century, emigrants from that region to South Russia quickly established vibrant autonomous colonies in which education became a central concern. By the end of the century, Mennonites in Russia had developed an elaborate system of village schools, supported by a teacher-training college, and supplemented by several vocational schools and even a specialized school for the blind and deaf.[9]

The first Mennonite immigrants to North America came out of the Swiss-South German tradition, settling in eastern Pennsylvania in the 1680s. Christopher Dock, an early Mennonite settler and schoolteacher in Germantown, wrote several well-known treatises on pedagogy and school management in the middle of the eighteenth century, making him one of the earliest published educational theorists in North America. But his work seems to have been an isolated exception. Most North American Mennonite families in the eighteenth and nineteenth centuries were content with an eighth-grade education in a local township school, which provided enough training to read the Scriptures and to succeed in the business demands of a farm economy.

Not until the second half of the nineteenth century did Mennonites in North America formally establish their first schools. In January of 1868, Carl Justus van der Smissen, a university-educated pastor from North Germany, with strong support from the Pennsylvania Mennonite leader John H. Oberholtzer, helped to launch the Wadsworth Institute in north-central Ohio. With an emphasis on biblical studies, the school operated for ten years before debts and low enrollment forced it to close. In 1887 the General Conference Mennonite Church established Bethel College in North Newton, Kansas, soon to be followed by Mennonite Collegiate Institute in Gretna, Manitoba (1889), Bluffton (Ohio) College (1898), and Freeman (SD) Junior College (1903). Then followed the emergence of several institutions closely associated with the Mennonite Church: Goshen (Ind) College (1903), Hesston (Kan) Academy (1909), and Eastern Mennonite College in Harrisonburg, Virginia (1917).

The real flurry of educational activity came in the middle decades of the twentieth century, especially at the elementary and secondary school level among Mennonite Church congregations and conferences in the eastern United States. The creation of the Greenwood Mennonite School in 1928 marked the beginning of a period of rapid growth in Mennonite church-related schools. Between 1940 and 1960 alone, Mennonites in the United States established no fewer than 25 elementary and secondary schools. By the beginning of the twenty-first century, 45 schools—including three seminaries and five colleges or universities—were affiliated in some way with Mennonite Education Agency of the newly created Mennonite Church USA.

The overall character of this period of rapid expansion can be summarized by considering four general themes.

Mennonite Schools: Date of Founding by Decade	
1880–1889:	1
1890–1899:	1
1900–1909:	3
1910–1919:	2
1920–1929:	1
1930–1939:	1
1940–1949:	14
1950–1959:	11
1960–1969:	4
1970–1979:	2
1980–1989:	3
1990–1999:	2
2000–2010:	2

Local and Unsystematic Beginnings: Wide Variations in Ownership and Control

First, the flourishing of Mennonite schools in North America was not the result of a coordinated denominational effort arising out of a central organizational structure or rooted in a unified theology or pedagogy. By the mid-twentieth century, Mennonites throughout the church were expressing strong interest in the question of education. According to Donald Kraybill, a prominent Mennonite sociologist, nearly a hundred articles on the topic of Christian education appeared in the Mennonite denominational periodical, *Gospel Herald*, between 1942 and 1950.[10] The actual formation of Mennonite schools reflected quite a variety of local settings and circumstances.

Not surprisingly, the schools differed widely in terms of governance structures, curricular emphases, financial stability, and local support. A few schools, like Greenwood Mennonite, began at the initiative of a single congregation. More commonly, especially among the many elementary schools established by Mennonites in the East, schools were organized by parent- or patron-controlled boards, with strong financial support from local congregations, often in the form of annual contributions or regular fundraisers.

Most of the Mennonite high schools, by contrast, were originally established by regional conferences, though the nature of conference financial support and administrative oversight ranged widely from school to school. In more recent years, several urban schools—including the Chicago (Ill.) Mennonite Learning Center (1981–2008), Philadelphia (Pa.) Mennonite High School (1998), Hopedale (Ill.) Christian Life Academy (2008), and Peace and Justice Academy in Pasadena, California (2009)—emerged as cooperative ventures, drawing on the combined support of regional conferences, local congregations, and committed patrons.

Preserving the Faith (and Culture): The Defensive Character of Mennonite Education

One theme shared by many schools founded in the mid-twentieth century was a concern to preserve the distinctive character of Mennonite faith and practice in the face of powerful pressures for cultural assimilation. During the first half of the twentieth century, educational reformers throughout the United States eagerly set about to consolidate the scattered one-room rural schoolhouses, along with small-town elementary and high schools, into larger centralized schools. Consolidation promised improved facilities, winning sports teams, and greater efficiencies. But it also disrupted the local ties and intimate relationships that gave smaller communities their distinctive identity. Children now rode buses to school instead of walking. Control of school boards shifted from parents to highly educated specialists. State officials took a more active hand in standardizing curriculum.

At the same time, World War II marked a period of intense patriotism in the United States that heightened tensions between the local community and Mennonites because of their commitment to nonresistance. Pressure to support the war effort was powerful at every level of society but especially among young men of draft age who were just completing high school. When Mennonite church leaders realized after the war that nearly 58 percent of young men in the General Conference Mennonite Church and 30 percent in the Mennonite Church had joined the military, they were forced to acknowledge that the biblical and theological foundations of nonresistance had not been adequately communicated to Mennonite youth.[11] In their judgment, the Christian training that occurred in congregations and families was no longer sufficiently preparing young people to withstand the pressures to conform to mainstream American culture.

In response to these new realities, church leaders in many Mennonite communities, especially in the (Old) Mennonite Church, began to organize church-based schools as a response to the threat of cultural accommodation and theological drift. Indeed, many of the Mennonite elementary and high schools established during the 1940s and 1950s consciously sought to promote Mennonite theological convictions in the face of the culture of nationalism and militarism so evident in public education during the war years. They also promised to defend traditional Mennonite cultural markers that seemed to be under siege by the growing influence of mass media and the increased mobility afforded by access to cars and cheap transportation. Mennonite schools became havens against the threat of cultural accommodation and offered safe harbors for Mennonite youth in an increasingly turbulent society.

Patrons of the schools hoped their children would be well educated in these new institutions and fully prepared to enter the work world or even to go on to college. But their paramount concern was to create a setting for young people that would nurture, preserve, and reinforce the distinctive beliefs of the Mennonite faith and the inherited practices of Mennonite community life.

For much of the twentieth century, this was the dominant model of Mennonite education: In the face of political, economic, and culture changes eroding the tightly knit agrarian relationships of traditional Mennonite communities, the new schools would help churches and young people rediscover Christ's call to peacemaking while also protecting Mennonite youth against the pressures of acculturation. In 1978 Donald Kraybill made this goal explicit in *Mennonite Education: Issues, Facts, and Changes*. "As the old meanings of Mennonite identity, forged in our rural experience, fade away," he wrote, Mennonite schools will be necessary "to identify and transmit the more symbolic glue which will bind us together in the future."[12]

Although some readers may find this model of Christian education to be overly defensive or sectarian, if not naive or quaint, Mennonites were by no means unique in this understanding. A concern to preserve a distinctive understanding of faith and practice in the face of a secularizing culture characterized virtually all faith-based schools in the twentieth century, whether they were Catholic, Jewish, Reformed, or Lutheran. And since religious convictions are never expressed apart from specific ritual and cultural practices, the ethnic component of these church-based schools—things like the desire to promote intermarriage while preserving a distinctive language, folkways, and collective memories—was almost inseparable from the more explicitly religious goals. Thus Catholic schools in urban Italian neighborhoods embraced Italian culture. Lutheran schools in Swedish communities celebrated Swedish folkways and customs. Reformed schools in Michigan wove together family networks with a shared Dutch genealogy. And Jewish schools in New York City sought to preserve a language and culture without which the faith was almost impossible to imagine.

So the impulse of the Greenwood Mennonite congregation and dozens of other Mennonite communities to establish schools to sustain a culturally infused religious faith in the face of the homogenizing forces of American culture was not unique. Today this preservationist model of church-related education continues to be a powerful force for a large network of Amish, Old Order Mennonite, and other conservative Mennonite parochial schools along with hundreds of Baptist, fundamentalist, and nondenominational schools.

Movement Toward Professionalization/Institutionalization

Almost all of the histories of the Mennonite elementary and secondary schools that started in the 1940s and 1950s follow a similar story line. Most of them begin with a narrative of a humble but heroic birth. Virtually all Mennonite schools started on a shoestring budget and with the most rudimentary of facilities. Heavily dependent on volunteer labor, they were often led by a staff whose commitment to the cause outweighed their formal credentials. Although the early chapters of those histories highlight the vision, zeal, and generous financial support of a few key individuals, the success of the schools depended on a broad community of support. Local pastors frequently served as the first administrators. Parents filled in as cooks and bus drivers. Athletic teams, if they existed at all, practiced in pastures or rented local gyms. The lingering memories of the early years are those of a collective commitment to a shared cause—"This is our school!"—and a local pride in pressing ahead under extremely adverse circumstances.

The next chapters of the institutional histories tell a story of growing stability. Out of humble and ad hoc beginnings, the schools charted a steady path toward institutional maturity. Although several schools were accredited from the beginning, most found their way only gradually to formal accreditation, which often meant that teachers and administrators were required to seek appropriate certification, the curriculum had to meet state standards, and the school needed to add a substantial library. Over time parents expected higher standards of technology, which brought the addition of media centers and computer labs. As athletics became more significant, schools joined conferences that also had minimum requirements for playing fields, uniforms, paid referees, lights for night games, and seating capacity for fans. All of these improvements cost money. Gradually schools came to employ full-time development staff, who introduced newsletters, annual fundraisers, and strategic planning, while bringing new attentiveness to alumni relations and to cultivating donors.

In some ways these transitions were inevitable and signs of institutional maturity. Yet greater professionalization and organizational sophistication meant that relations with core constituents would be renegotiated. For example, whereas schools were once assumed to be fully aligned with congregational standards on nonconformity—things like dress codes, devotional coverings, or restrictions on movie attendance—by the end of the twentieth century it became clear that schools were no longer children of the conference or congregations, but independent entities. Some boards promoted the idea of an endowment to provide for long-term financial stability, independent of a direct reliance on local churches for the annual budget. Board members attending seminars on fundraising learned the 90-10 (or 95-5) rule, in which 90 percent of the money is contributed by 10 percent of the people—meaning that their relational focus turned increasingly to the wealthy. Enrollment pressures brought higher expectations for gleaming facilities—not just classrooms, but also science labs, performing arts centers, chapels, and gymnasiums. And schools struggled to negotiate the widening differences in parental assumptions and congregational expectations regarding acceptable student behavior or orthodox teaching in Bible class.

Although this description may sound negative, many Mennonite schools flourished during the 1970s and 1980s. As enrollment expanded, they embarked on impressive capital campaigns, incorporated service-learning and intercultural experiences into the curriculum, made their mark in athletics, and gained strong reputations for the quality of their academic and music programs.

Broadened Mission and New Visions

During the second half of the twentieth century, this transformation in many Mennonite schools—moving from local initiatives built on close personal ties with local community members and congregations to more formal institutions with rationalized administrative procedures and a greater sense of independence—inevitably suggested a shift in institutional mission. As each school's constituency base broadened, new questions of mission and identity needed to be addressed. Some boards did so in careful and deliberate fashion, drawing on the resources of the Mennonite Board of Education of the Mennonite Church or the General Conference's Commission on Education. But many schools simply adjusted their programs in response to shifting market realities, generally resulting in looser connections to local Mennonite congregations and conferences.

Today the idea that Mennonite schools exist primarily to protect Mennonite young people from the cultural influences of the broader society has been rendered obsolete. Almost all contemporary Mennonite schools—elementary, secondary, college, and seminary—now serve significantly different student bodies than they did when they were founded.[13] In 1950, Mennonite students often comprised 90 percent to 100 percent of the student body; by the turn of the century that number had dropped to 50 percent in many schools, and in some schools to less than 20 percent.

As the percentage of students from Mennonite homes steadily declined, schools broadened their recruitment base to include students from a broad range of religious traditions or from no religious tradition at all. Only in rare cases was this shift the result of a conscious, strategic decision. More frequently it reflected the slow but inexorable consequences of a decline in Mennonite family size, coupled with waning support for Mennonite education in local congregations, and conversely, a growing demand among other people in the community for a church-related alternative to the public school.

Parallel to this shift in the religious composition of students, school boards and administrators have slowly begun to articulate a broader understanding of the mission of church-based Mennonite education. Increasingly, Mennonite schools and universities find themselves obliged to demonstrate equal if not superior academic standards, quality of facilities, and extracurricular opportunities as other schools, while also providing faith-based instruction for a diverse student body. Today supporters of Mennonite educational institutions describe the mission of the school in terms of educational excellence, alongside a general foundation in faith values and a broad-minded commitment to service.

The newest MEA-affiliated schools are emerging in urban settings, far from areas where Mennonites have traditionally settled and without the cultural assumptions that gave rise to the flurry of schools established in the 1950s and 1960s. Deeply shaped by Anabaptist-Mennonite theology, the educational entrepreneurs who have planted these schools are excited about creating educational alternatives to both public school and standard Christian school options. Most of these fledgling initiatives do not look—on the surface at least—at all like the traditional model I have been describing. Almost all are located in urban settings and have students representing many cultures. Their local supporters are often deeply interested in Anabaptist-Mennonite theology and practices but not necessarily committed to the tradition.

These new schools point to an emerging model of Mennonite education that is likely to expand in the future. The full shape of that new model is not yet clearly known; indeed, many questions remain to be resolved. But it does seem clear that the future of Mennonite education will be more culturally and religiously diverse, more missional in its orientation, and more dynamic in its adjustments to shifting economic realities.

Conclusion

Given the significant transformation long underway in Mennonite schools, a fresh discussion of the underlying philosophy of church-related education is clearly in order.

Today, more than ever before, Mennonites in North America are deeply integrated into the public life of their local communities. They pay taxes that support local schools. And they work as public school administrators, teachers, and staff members. They participate in local service clubs and community business associations. Immersed in a world that often regards support for local public schools as a measure of civic responsibility and good citizenship, many Mennonites are no longer persuaded that the value added by sending their children to a Mennonite school is significant enough to make it worth the price of tuition dollars.

Yet the Mennonite church continues to be heavily invested in church-sponsored education. In the midst of a dynamic context—shaped by challenging economic realities, shifting market demands, uncertain theological commitments, and a denominational identity in flux—families and congregations will need to address a host of questions about the future of church-based education: What are our fundamental goals in the education of our children? How are our religious convictions relevant to these goals? In our enlightened, democratic society, do we need church-sponsored schools? What is the distinctive mission of Anabaptist Mennonite schools? What would an education shaped by Anabaptist-Mennonite theology look like? What, if anything, do all the schools under the MEA umbrella hold in common?

In the following chapters, I address these questions by sketching the outlines of a philosophy of Christian education in an Anabaptist-Mennonite perspective. What follows is not a formulaic definition or a packaged program. Rather, I offer an overview of Anabaptist-Mennonite theology and describe the outlines of a pedagogy consistent with that theology. I conclude with a proposed set of outcomes that schools shaped by the Anabaptist-Mennonite tradition might expect to find in all their students.

The conversation that follows does not resolve the many questions confronting Mennonite education today, but I trust that it will enliven that discussion and focus the debate in a constructive way.

2

Theological Starting Points:
The Incarnation as the Foundation of Anabaptist-Mennonite Education

In the months that followed the devastating attacks on New York City's Twin Towers in September 2001, the mood of the nation was understandably agitated. One expression of national outrage took the form of spontaneous displays of patriotic unity. American flags appeared on porches and along streets. Schoolchildren and civic groups recited the Pledge of Allegiance with new fervor. Armed Forces representatives became much more visible during the singing of the national anthem before sporting events. These symbols underscored a new national readiness to go to war against those responsible for the terrorist attacks.

Amid this national outpouring of patriotic sentiment, the tradition of several Mennonite schools to not sing the national anthem, fly the American flag, or pledge allegiance to the flag triggered renewed criticism from local communities. Public concerns ranged from bafflement to indignant outrage: Why would you not affirm the sentiments of the nation at a time of crisis? Do you hate your country? Are you ungrateful to the military? Do you support terrorism? For many in the community, the hesitancy of these schools to join public displays of nationalism—however long-standing those policies may have been—seemed callous and arrogant, out of touch with the hard realities of violence.

The new national mood following September 11 posed a real quandary for some Mennonite school boards and administrators. In the face of public criticism and the decision of some parents to withdraw their students, school officials in several communities tried to explain their position in local newspapers, albeit with limited success. For virtually all Mennonite schools, the moment led to a vigorous internal debate and a fresh consideration of traditional assumptions: What is the relationship between allegiance to Jesus and allegiance to the nation? How can we more effectively communicate our convictions with the broader community? Are these policies worth the cost in public relations? Do we actually believe in them ourselves?

Although the debate was not always pleasant and still remains unresolved, it did prompt an important conversation about identity, mission, and the theological foundations of Mennonite education. Just what does it mean to be a school in the Anabaptist-Mennonite tradition? What Christian convictions are central to the identity and character of those schools affiliated with the Mennonite Education Agency? How should those convictions be best expressed? On what points should Mennonite schools consciously align themselves with the broader Christian community—emphasizing their commonalities with Christians from a variety of denominations—and at what points should Mennonite schools openly declare, defend, and promote those distinctive characteristics that set them apart?

The issues at stake go far beyond questions of nationalism and public symbols of patriotic unity. As I suggest in this chapter, this is only one of many ways that a distinctive Anabaptist-Mennonite theology might take on visible expression. But the issues swirling around flags, pledges, and national anthems do helpfully focus the larger theological framework that characterizes an Anabaptist-Mennonite approach to education.

Mennonite Theology and the Embarrassment of Particularity

When many of us think about the word *theology*, one image that comes quickly to mind is a stack of thick books laden with arguments about the nature of God, filled with lots of Scripture references and tedious debates among scholars, most of whom are long since dead. For others, theology means a specific set of doctrines, issued by church leaders or anchored in long-standing tradition, that we absolutely have to believe if we are going to call ourselves Christians. For still others, theology evokes ideas more abstract and cerebral—reflections on the nature of love or philosophical musing about concepts like spirituality or truth.

If any of these are your beginning point for a discussion of theology, then the Anabaptist-Mennonite approach to the subject may seem confusing and even a bit frustrating. In contrast to many other Christian traditions, Mennonites have not generally defined themselves in terms of an authoritative confession of faith or by a clearly delineated structure of church hierarchy. Unlike Lutherans, for example, Mennonites do not have an unchanging historical confession of faith that has remained firmly in place since the sixteenth century. Nor do Mennonites have a pope, like the Catholic tradition, who speaks with absolute authority on theological matters from the center of the church. In contrast to the Reformed tradition, Mennonites have not generally expressed their convictions in systematic arguments or with the tight logical rigor of John Calvin's *Institutes*. Indeed, the Mennonite tendency to value local discernment of Scripture at the congregational or conference level has sometimes made it difficult to summarize the Mennonite position on controversial theological matters, so that even within the organizational structure of Mennonite Church USA, regional differences and local traditions have led the schools affiliated with Mennonite Education Agency to embrace a variety of theological emphases.

These challenges have been complicated even further by the more recent tendency of many schools to broaden their base of constituent support beyond the Mennonite church. Many Mennonite schools, as we have noted, trace their origins to a moment in the history of their local communities when it seemed as if the distinctive markers of Mennonite identity were eroding. A primary task of Mennonite schools was to preserve the theological convictions, cultural habits, and ethical practices that had traditionally separated Mennonites from the surrounding culture. Today that model of defensive insularity has largely broken down. Most Mennonite educational institutions now serve diverse student populations, whose interests are not primarily focused on shoring up Mennonite communal identity. And schools are increasingly dependent on the tuition income that these diverse students bring.

Even as this shift in orientation has provided Mennonite schools with welcome new opportunities for missional outreach, it has also complicated the internal conversation about theological identity. Given the increasing diversity of its constituency, Mennonite schools today struggle with what might be called the "embarrassment of particularity." They fear that claiming a distinctive theological identity too explicitly will be perceived by others as inhospitable or arrogant. Even worse, highlighting a distinctive theological identity might be seen as a reversion to the older sectarian model of defensive ethnicity, making it difficult for students and faculty who have not been raised within a traditional Mennonite community to feel like they truly belong.

At its best, the growing diversity in Mennonite schools has prompted school administrators, teachers, and supporters to reflect more intentionally on basic theological convictions and to be more explicit about how those convictions find expression in the day-to-day life of the institution. Regular interaction with students and parents from many theological traditions encourages an institution to be more explicit about its core values and more conscious about communicating those convictions in a gracious and inviting way.

At its worst, the new missional mode of many Anabaptist-Mennonite educational institutions has opened the door to theological confusion. In an effort to avoid the embarrassment of particularity, some boards and administrators are tempted to minimize all theological differences that might set their school apart in any way from the larger Protestant or evangelical tradition.

Often the reaction against the embarrassment of particularity happens gradually and innocently, more a result of inattentiveness than as a conscious strategy. Schools that began with the strong support of local Mennonite congregations, for example, may observe that their initial enthusiasm is slowly ebbing. Perhaps some congregations have withdrawn their support, upset that the school has not adequately embraced broader currents of evangelical piety or worship styles. For others, rising tuition costs may have prompted some longtime supporters to reconsider the public school option.

Faced with the reality of declining enrollment and the prospects of even higher tuition, boards begin to feel pressure to make the school more attractive to a broader market, which could include *all* Christian groups in the community, or to appeal to those who have no interest in the Christian faith but are simply looking for a good educational alternative to the public school.

Sometimes it happens that school board members or administrators have themselves experienced deep spiritual blessings from the ministry of Christian radio or television programs outside the Mennonite mainstream. Or they have attended seminars sponsored by nondenominational organizations or participated in conferences where dynamic speakers describe the future of Christian education from their own theological perspectives. As these same administrators represent the school to prospective families not connected with a Mennonite congregation, it may feel natural to emphasize the points of commonality with the broader Christian tradition rather than to highlight Mennonite distinctives. As a result, boards, administrators, staff, and teachers gradually find themselves explaining the character of the school in generic terms: "Mennonites pretty much believe all the same things as other Protestants. Yes, they do have a few quirky additional practices, but we do not emphasize these, and they should not get in the way of your support of the school."

Over time, the school's culture reflects these assumptions. New teachers are hired on the basis of generally shared Christian convictions. Chapel speakers reflect the full theological or denominational diversity of the student body. New emphases of identity emerge—claiming, for example, that "We are all Christians," or "We are all Americans, or "We are all defenders of democracy"— that seem more compatible with attitudes shared by the broader community.

The positive side of this approach is that it is warm and expansive, openly embracing other evangelical Christians by emphasizing points of commonality and by being flexible about distinctive beliefs and practices that have in the past separated Mennonites and other groups. After all, Anabaptist-Mennonite groups hold many of the same orthodox convictions that one would find in all Christian groups: a high view of Scripture, an affirmation of the Trinity, a sober understanding of the reality of sin, a recognition that salvation rests on the gift of God's grace, and a conviction that God is active in history and will someday restore creation to its intended purpose. In this sense, Mennonites are not a sect or a cult, nor are they separatist followers of the secret revelations of an eccentric individual. After spending so much energy during past years in distancing themselves from other groups—defining their identity in the negative terms of what they were *not*—it is healthy for Mennonites to recognize a greater degree of commonality and fellowship with Christians across a broad spectrum of the church. The new posture of Mennonite education that embraces a more diverse group of teachers, students, and supporters should be regarded as a sign of renewal and a gift of God's grace, offering new opportunities to share the good news freely and to be transformed by the Spirit.

Yet even as board members, administrators, and teachers in Mennonite schools negotiate these new realities, they would do well to keep in mind several basic principles.

1. Every School Has an Identity: There's No Escaping the "Embarrassment of Particularity"

The first principle is really quite simple. Having a distinctive identity is not a choice; it is a reality. Your school, even if claims to be nondenominational or simply Christian, will always reflect a *particular* theological and cultural identity. Every school, for example, will have glossy brochures and other advertising material describing the qualities that make the school distinctive. Every school will have a mission statement that defines its priorities and goals. Every school will have a set of policies regarding whom it hires and the standards of performance and behavior it expects from its employees. Every school will have a budget in which it prioritizes some programs above others. And every Christian school will have some statement of faith that defines the boundaries of acceptable theological teaching and moral behavior.

Beyond all of this, every school will also have an informal or unofficial culture—a reputation or a certain feel that will make some new students feel very welcome and will likely signal to others that they probably are not a good fit for the school.

On the surface, all this may be obvious. But sometimes in the context of Mennonite schools, the rejection of a particular identity inherited from the past is defended with arguments suggesting that particularity itself is the problem. This is the logic at work, for example, when people say, "Because Mennonite distinctives have been so exclusive, let's just be a Christian school." In fact, being "just Christian" is an impossibility. If yours is not a Mennonite school, then it will simply be a different kind of school, but no less particular in its identity. The school will *always* express its identity in specific ways that ultimately exclude as much as they include.

In this sense, schools that claim to be nondenominational or generically Christian are no different, in principle, from schools that are clear from the start about their distinctive qualities. Since it is impossible to escape the particularity of belief, rather than pretending to be nondenominational, it would be much better to be self-conscious, thoughtful, and clear about your school's convictions and to offer gracious explanations as to why you hold them.

Thus the crucial issue for thoughtful board members and administrators should not be how to avoid the embarrassment of particularity, but rather what *kind* of particular identity they want to affirm for the school and how to best express it.

2. Because Identity Is Always Particular, Christian Schools Should Know Their Traditions

To say that all identity is "particular" might sound like it is random or arbitrary, which is emphatically not the case. Behind healthy identity is the gift of a story—our theological beliefs and practices are always rooted in a deeper tradition. A tradition offers a frame of reference that gives meaning and coherence to the many choices that structure our lives. To know our traditions is to have a place to stand in the midst of a complex and rapidly changing world. Indeed, if the distinctive beliefs and practices of a church-related school are to be preserved, renewed, challenged, and shared, then schools need to be very conscious and intentional about the traditions that give rise to them.

No one should be surprised, for example, to discover that the local Jewish school focuses a great deal of attention on the Hebrew language and Hebrew Scriptures, or that it would celebrate distinctive Jewish holidays or refuse to schedule athletic events on the Sabbath. Catholics in North America may not always fully agree with the pope, but no one attending the University of Notre Dame would be shocked to discover daily mass offered in the dorms, to hear references to the Virgin Mary, or to encounter theology classes devoted to Catholic teachings. Not all groups in the Reformed tradition see eye to eye on every point of doctrine, yet the writings of Calvin and basic understandings about the sovereignty of God or the limits to free will provide a reference point for thinking about the theological themes one expects at a Reformed school. All Lutheran schools are anchored—whether explicitly or not—in an understanding of Scripture read through the lens of the Augsburg Confession. Indeed, one can legitimately ask why any group would expend the considerable energy and resources that go into private, church-related education if there is no identifiable theological tradition to support the school's practices, emphases, and character.

Thus every Christian school will not only have a particular identity, it will also need to be attentive to the deeper traditions that shape the theological convictions, ethical practices, and worship styles that give that identity its integrity and coherence.

3. Knowing Your Tradition Is a Key to Missions, Not an Obstacle

Thus far I have suggested that a particular identity informed by a deeper theological tradition is unavoidable, even among schools that claim to be nondenominational. The concern, of course, is that this emphasis on particularity and tradition—especially in a Mennonite context—will only reinforce the defensiveness of the past and ultimately hinder mission. Yet consciously embracing the distinctive themes of Anabaptist-Mennonite theology might actually serve as a path to mission rather than an obstacle.

The tendency of some Mennonite groups to focus primarily on the boundaries that separate themselves from the rest of the Christian world has indeed led to problems. A negative form of identity, dependent on having enemies so we can know who we are *not*, is fraught with various forms of arrogance and legalism and can foster endless divisions in a quest for doctrinal or ethical purity. But the bigger challenge today for most Mennonites is precisely the opposite. In a well-intended effort to avoid a theological identity that might be perceived as unwelcoming, sectarian, or irrelevant, the end result for many schools has generally not been a stronger missional outreach, but rather theological confusion.

This dilemma raises basic questions about the nature of mission that are worth exploring. Since the Enlightenment of the eighteenth century, most educated Christians have struggled with the recognition that any individual claim regarding the truth—especially religious truth—has been conditioned in some way by a particular culture, the accident of birth into a particular family, or the unique circumstances shaping one's perspective. What I think of as a universal truth might actually only be the product of my local, limited point of view.

For Christians who recognize the profound consequences of this realization, the missionary challenge becomes acute. How am I to persuade anyone else—strangers on the other side of the world, our next-door neighbors, or even my own children—about the good news of the gospel if my understandings of God are merely a product of my particular culture? One response, especially in the Catholic, Reformed, and some evangelical traditions, is to appeal to reason. We avoid the embarrassment of particularity by arguing for the faith on the basis of universal reason. If one begins with the assumption that theology is mostly about what happens in our minds—about believing the right things or arguing our way back to God—then the task of Christian educators is to present Christian beliefs as a coherent intellectual system, using all the rigorous arguments, rational evidence, and tight logic that we can muster. By careful argumentation we reveal the inconsistencies of atheism or agnosticism, and we persuade our conversation partners to recognize the truth of the Christian gospel.

Unfortunately, most people are not likely to be won over by this approach. Indeed, what we are used to calling theology is rarely as conscious or as cerebral as we seem to assume. Though theology technically means "words about God," at a deeper level it really points to our most foundational assumptions about the nature of the world. Sometimes we are able to formulate our beliefs in tidy sentences. But often our theology goes far beyond explicit doctrinal statements that can be listed like a legal contract ("I believe x, y, and z").

Our theology touches on our deepest fears, hopes, and desires: attitudes that we bring to the world without a fully developed rationale. It is a fairly simple matter, for example, to say that the Bible is the "plenary, inspired, inerrant Word of God" or that "Jesus died for my sins." But the hopes, fears, attitudes, and desires that actually shape our daily decisions are probably a more accurate window into our theology than abstract statements or lists of doctrinal affirmations. In fact, the truest expression of what we actually believe can be found in our habits, practices, assumptions, and inclinations—the things we say and do in the daily routines of life that greatly affect how we react when life confronts us with profound surprises and our familiar rhythms are challenged.

In the end, what we truly believe will be made evident in how we live. Ultimately, Christian conversion is not so much a matter of rational thought and logical persuasion as it is a transformation of the heart—a reorientation of our desires, habits, and practices that turns us toward the worship of God rather than the worship of ourselves.

Our recognition that Christian theology touches something deeper than intellectual arguments or doctrinal beliefs has important implications for how we communicate our faith—what is often described as "mission." It also has important implications for how we think about pedagogy.

❦

A distinctive identity, shaped by a conscious engagement with a theological tradition, is crucial to mission. Authentic mission is less a matter of presenting the gospel in general and generic language, than it is about communicating convictions in a gracious, clear manner, and then living a life that reflects those convictions in a consistent way. What would this look like in the Anabaptist-Mennonite tradition?

The Word Made Flesh: The Incarnation as the Key to Anabaptist-Mennonite Theology

At the heart of all theological reflection is a question that humans have pondered since the beginning of time: How do heaven and earth meet? How does the transcendent world of the Spirit intersect with the ordinary material world of time and space? In short, how are humans reconciled with God?

Through the centuries, Christians in various traditions have answered this question in many different ways. Most Protestants describe salvation through the doctrine of the atonement—focusing especially on the crucifixion of Jesus—with particular emphasis on themes like blood, sacrifice, forgiveness, and grace. In its briefest form, Jesus died for our sins. Through the shedding of his innocent blood, Christ paid the debt of our sins. All we need to do is to accept this gift by inviting Jesus into our hearts as our Lord and personal Savior. For many Christians, these phrases are so familiar that we scarcely give them a second thought. This is the formula for salvation; everything else that follows in terms of belief or practice is secondary.

Those in the Anabaptist-Mennonite tradition have generally understood salvation in a somewhat different way. It is not that we think Jesus is unimportant to Christian conversion. To the contrary. Mennonites strongly affirm that in the person of Jesus Christ, heaven and earth meet, and humans are reconciled with God and with each other. Virtually all Mennonite schools proclaim in their mission or vision statement that they are "Christ-centered." But the primary emphasis within the Anabaptist-Mennonite tradition has not been focused so much on the blood sacrifice of Jesus death as it has been on his life, teachings, death, and resurrection. Above all, the Anabaptist focus has been on the incarnation: Jesus is God *incarnate*, which means "in the flesh." Jesus is the Word made flesh. Jesus is the bridge that unites creation with its Creator. In Jesus, the world has been given the fullest revelation of God's purposes and intention for creation. In Jesus, we have an authoritative model for how to live. In Jesus, we find our salvation.

The incarnation underscores the divine authority of Jesus: In the person of Jesus, God is made visible to humanity. "In the beginning," writes the apostle John in the opening of his Gospel, "was the Word, and the word was with God, and the word was God. . . . and the Word [referring here to Jesus] was made flesh" (John 1:1, 14 KJV). "Whoever has seen me," Jesus tells an astonished crowd of listeners, "has seen the Father . . . who sent me" (John 14:9, 24 NRSV). For those who still have doubts, Jesus goes straight to the point: "I and the Father are one" (John 10:30).

This is a stunning claim! Jesus is not a god or a metaphor for God, or a lot like God. No, Jesus is God in human form. In the flesh-and-blood body of Jesus, God has become one with humanity. The consequences for Christian salvation and the nature of the Christian life that follow from this focus on the incarnation are profound.

It is significant, for example, that the biblical account of the incarnation—the Word made Flesh—begins not with the Gospels but with the story of creation itself. God's nature and character have always been revealed through the material world. Thus in the opening verses of the Bible, we discover that God is an active, living presence *within* creation from the very beginning of time. As God divides light from darkness, separates dry land from the waters, and creates plants and animals, God's spirit enters into the very stuff of creation itself. In a dramatic culminating act on the sixth day, God shapes a human form out of the dust of the earth, molds it in God's own image, and breathes into the nostrils of that form the very breath of life—the gift of a living spirit. From the beginning, God has created humans as incarnated beings—as ensouled bodies and embodied souls. And it was precisely this fusion of the created material world with the breath of God's Spirit that God pronounces to be "good."

Moreover, the opening chapters of Genesis make it clear that God has designed humans to live undivided lives. God's original intention for Adam and Eve in the garden of Eden is to live in relationships that are harmonious, trusting, transparent. Thus Adam and Eve walk with God in the cool of the day without any fear. They are naked to each other, without any embarrassment or shame. They live at peace with the natural world.

Unfortunately, the reality of sin shatters this blissful image. The consequences of sin, as described in Genesis 3, are clear. What God intended to be united is now divided. Because of sin, humans are separated from God (Adam and Eve hide when God walks with them). Because of sin, humans are now at odds with each other (Adam and Eve wear clothes to cover up parts of themselves; Cain kills Abel). And because of sin, humans are at odds with creation itself (now humans must sweat to secure their food; they struggle against thorns and snakes).

Because the unity of spirit and flesh that God has intended for creation has been severed, human beings begin to regard the creation as a mere object or a thing. This is most evident in the human impulse to construct idols—the human tendency to worship things *we* have created rather than the Creator. But it is also evident in the human impulse to treat other human beings as mere things: as objects of lust, as means to our own ends, or, even worse, as mere bodies that can be killed if they stand in our way. The same temptation is revealed in our attitude toward nature and our inclination to treat creation as if it were a mere commodity. All these human tendencies are the consequences of sin, the lingering evidence of the fall.

Yet the fall is only the prelude for an even grander story still to follow. God's creative work is not done! Sin has divided us from God, from each other, and from creation, but the rest of the Bible is a long account of God's patient and persistent calling of humanity back to the wholeness and harmony for which we were intended. God is never distant or aloof from creation. Indeed, throughout the Hebrew Scriptures, God is always made visible in material, tangible, and physical ways: a bush that burns, waters that part at the right moment, manna that falls miraculously from heaven, commandments physically inscribed in stone, the ark of the covenant that holds mysterious powers, a temple in which God is said to dwell.

God is also made visible in human history through the witness of a tiny nomadic people who are called out to reveal God's character and original intention for humanity—to reveal God's will to all the nations. The stories of God's mighty acts in history—through Abraham, Sarah, Miriam, Moses, David, Daniel, and Esther—reveal a God of justice and mercy, of power and compassion, of righteousness and love. The prophets of Israel believed that God's revelation in history was still not complete. They yearned for the "healing of the nations"—for a time when the lion and the lamb shall live in harmony, and no one shall be afraid (cf. Rev 22:2; Isa 11:6-9; 65:25). They prayed fervently for the day when the whole earth would be "filled with the . . . glory of the LORD, as the waters cover the sea" (Hab 2:14 NRSV), or a time to come when "all flesh" shall behold the glory of God (Isa 40:5 KJV). Above all, they looked forward to the full revelation of God in the form of the Anointed or Blessed One, the Messiah.

In Jesus, heaven and earth were literally joined. In Jesus, creation is being restored to God's original intention for all of humanity.

The Gospels make it clear that Jesus was a physical human being. He was born to real parents in the village of Bethlehem at the time when Quirinius governed Syria, and he was part of a long genealogical heritage that goes all the way back to David. The Gospels describe Jesus as a real flesh-and-blood person who shared every aspect of ordinary human life. He ate, slept, and drank. He wept when he heard of Lazarus's death. He got mad at the buyers and sellers in the temple. He struggled to control his fear in the garden of Gethsemane. He experienced the anguish of loneliness and rejection. He suffered intense physical pain. And he died a humiliating and painful death.

Yet at the same time, Jesus was not just another human being. After all, he was born to a virgin. Nature itself celebrated his birth in the form of a star. Choirs of celestial angels stunned shepherds with hymns of praise. Throughout his ministry, Jesus consistently blurred the divide between the physical and the spiritual world. He performed miracles of physical healing. He calmed storms. He cast out demons. He fed whole crowds with a few fishes and loaves of bread. He raised the dead to life again. In the end, not even death itself could claim the final word. After three days in the grave, Christ was raised from the dead, ministered to his disciples for another forty days, and then ascended into heaven.

The human inclination has always been to pull apart the mystery of the incarnation. We are often inclined to turn Jesus into a cosmic Savior who did not really have a body, or we want to reduce Jesus to a really good human being, a humanitarian hero, but not someone to be confused with God. Yet the Bible and Christian tradition will not let us get away with that. The reality of the incarnation forces us to live with the paradox that an infinite God is revealed to humanity within the finite form of a physical body.

◁◁◁

These thoughts on the incarnation might seem far removed from the institutional realities of a school administrator or the daily activities of a classroom teacher. Yet, for educators the consequences of an incarnational theology are profound. In later chapters, I will explore the significance of the incarnation for pedagogy and educational outcomes in much greater detail. For the moment, however, I simply propose five specific consequences that this emphasis on the incarnation has had for the Anabaptist-Mennonite theological tradition.

1. Because of the Incarnation Creation Matters

A Christian pedagogy rooted in a theology of the incarnation will be attentive to the fact that the natural world is God's creation, not ours; that we are integrally connected with nature; and that, as stewards of that creation, we will engage the natural world with a posture of wonder, blessing, appreciation, and gentleness.

From the beginning, God's will and purposes have always been revealed in the material world, the physical reality of creation. When the Messiah arrived, he did so not as a spiritual abstraction, but in the tangible form of a real human being. This means that our bodies, limited and weak though they may be, are not intrinsically evil. Things of the flesh have the potential to do evil, but they also have the potential to reveal the very character of God. So how we treat our bodies, and how we treat the bodies of other people, is a crucial part of our Christian witness to the world.

In a similar way, salvation affects our relationship with the natural world. Some Christians have interpreted God's mandate to "rule" or to have "dominion over" the earth (Gen 1:26) as an argument for treating creation and its resources as things or objects fundamentally distinct from human beings. Because humans were created by God (rather than through evolution), the argument goes, and because human are to have "dominion over the earth" (and therefore a right to extract from it all they can), and because our true home is in heaven (rather than in the finite limitations of this earth), then it is logical to regard the natural world as something whose value for Christians is strictly utilitarian—merely a source of resources that humans need to thrive.

Recognizing the natural world as God's creation and taking seriously our relationship with creation is not the same as worshipping nature; nor does it suggest that humans should quit using natural resources. But just as God is seeking to redeem humanity from the consequences of the fall, God is also seeking to restore our relationship with creation back to its original wholeness, which God pronounced "good." Therefore, Christians will be actively engaged in the care for God's created world and ready to participate—even if symbolically or only on a small scale—in acts that help to heal our alienation from God's creation.

For the Christian educator, this means that the world of biology, geology, physics, astronomy, and chemistry; the study of the human body in all of its complexity; the layers of intricately connected ecological balances that sustain human life; the marvel of human inquiry that directs our attention to the natural world in all its wonder and complexity—all these are encounters latent with the possibility of God's revelation in creation.

2. Because of the Incarnation History Matters

Just as the incarnation affirms that God is present in creation, or space, so too Christians believe that God is revealed to humanity in history, or *time*. As in nature, the reality of the fall is a central feature of the Christian story: the stubborn presence of sin is all too evident in the pages of human history. Indeed, the record of the past is so bloody that it would be easy to assume that greed, selfishness, and violence are the very motor of human history: Human beings have always hidden from God, always been at war with each other, and always destroyed creation.

Yet Christians are heirs to a powerful story that challenges those assumptions. The deeper reality of human history is that we were created by a loving God to live with God, each other, and creation in relationships of trust and harmony. In fact, the whole of the biblical story is a record of a God who faithfully calls humans back to a way of living that is consistent with God's original intentions: to live in relationships of trust, harmony, and intimacy. We can never fully recover the perfection of Eden; that awaits the consummation of history. But the Bible records God's active intervention in history and invites humans to participate in the good news of the gospel by living in this deeper story—a counternarrative to that of the world—sustained by the living presence of the Holy Spirit.

The heart of the story is about God, the creator of the universe. But the details are always expressed in particular, concrete ways: in the response of Abraham and Sarah to God's call to put their trust in him; in the account of the exodus and the formation of the Jewish people, called out by God to be "a light to the nations"; in the gift of the covenant and law, summarized in the Ten Commandments; in the promise of the Messiah as recounted by the prophets; and above all in the person of Jesus Christ, the Messiah, whose life, teachings, death, and resurrection most fully reveal the nature of God.

The gift of Story—of God's active intervention in human history—continues with the formation of a new community in Jerusalem at Pentecost and in the long, tangled account of the early church and its successors. Anabaptist-Mennonites form only one small episode of this larger drama of the church made visible in the world. Yet the stories that we tell from that tradition—of freely sharing goods and possession; of a stubborn commitment to love even enemies; of joy in the face of martyrdom; of leaving hearth and home for the sake of the gospel—are part of this larger effort to give voice to the drama of the incarnation.

All of us live out the narratives that we hear around us. Stories are the means by which we make sense of the world. They give an account for how we and the world came into existence. They shape our understanding of what it means to be human. They orient us to what is true and right and good. It should not be surprising that children who are raised in families dominated by abuse, fear, and anger and whose stories are steeped in conflict, messages of failure, and experiences of misplaced trust will have a harder time forming relationships than children whose stories are permeated by love and fidelity. Nor should we be shocked that the subtle stories recounted in advertisements, movies, and popular culture shape our lives in powerful ways that we often scarcely recognize.

Precisely because we are so deeply shaped by the narratives around us, Christian educators must be extremely attentive to the stories they pass along to their students. Mennonite educators should regularly invite their students to picture themselves as part of God's Story—created by a loving God to live in intimate relationships with himself, with each other, and with creation; separated and divided by the reality of sin, but invited to participate with Christ in healing a fragmented world.

Students in Mennonite schools will learn how to

weave their own stories into the larger history of their own congregations, the long trajectory of church history, and beyond that, into the foundational narrative of God's active presence in the grand sweep of human history.

3. Because of the Incarnation Community Matters

Another way of talking about the relevance of the incarnation for Anabaptist-Mennonite theology is to ask *how* Jesus is made visible in the world today. For many Christians, Jesus came primarily to die for our sins. They say that what matters most is to "accept Jesus into your heart," and you will be saved; everything else is secondary to your "personal relationship" with Christ. Although the church provides a place to gather for worship, many contemporary Christians believe its main purpose is to "help me in my Christian journey." The primary focus of God's salvation—God's work in the world—is on the individual and what is happening in my "heart."

The Anabaptists of the sixteenth century had a somewhat different perspective on the role of Christ and the nature of salvation. In his life, teachings, death, and resurrection, Christ defeated the power of death and the forces that divide humans from each other. Wherever Jesus went, his ministry focused on themes of healing what had been broken, diseased, or divided. He did not so much invite people to accept him "into their hearts" as to accept the gift of physical or mental healing, to participate in acts of radical hospitality, and to share the love of God with others in risky and vulnerable ways.

Thus, to be "saved" for the early Anabaptists meant a transformation of heart, mind, and body that called followers of Jesus to live new relationships with others, making the incarnation—the Word made flesh—a living reality. "I am the vine; you are the branches," Jesus told his disciples. "If you remain in me and I in you, you will bear much fruit" (cf. John 15:5). The image here is that of a living organism, each part deeply connected to the other through a common dependence on the vine. And each actively bears visible fruit as evidence of its relationship to the living Christ.

Even though Christ is no longer physically present on earth, he is alive and visible in the world today wherever people gather in his name and are committed to live in these relationships (Matt 18:20). The sixteenth-century Anabaptist Pilgram Marpeck once described the church as the "prolongation of the incarnation." He meant that the incarnation was not an event that happened once upon a time. Rather, Jesus remains alive in the world today wherever faithful believers embody his teachings in their relationships with each other and with their neighbors.

In its life together, the early Anabaptists taught, the community of Christian believers proclaims to the world God's intention at creation for all humanity. In the Christian church resources were shared freely and sins openly confessed and forgiven. Here, those in authority did not lord over weaker members; barriers between Gentiles and Jews, slaves and free, men and women were broken down; and all people were to be treated with dignity and respect. This new community is the "body of Christ"—the "new creation" made visible to the world (2 Cor 5:17).

For Christian educators, this understanding of the gospel calls us to be attentive to our community life. How we treat each other may be as important to a faith-based education as the content of our doctrinal teachings or the expressiveness of our worship.

4. Because of the Incarnation Individuals Matter

A theology of incarnation reminds us that we were created for relationships and designed for community. Yet this does not mean that we forfeit our individuality or lose our identity. To the contrary, a Christian life shaped by the incarnation creates the possibility for truly authentic individual identity. In a culture that is deeply confused about what it means to be a whole person, Anabaptist-Mennonite schools will help students develop strong personal identities in which body, mind, and spirit are fully integrated.

As we have seen, one clear consequence of sin in the biblical account is the human impulse to separate and divide what God intended to be joined. This tendency is evident not only in human societies, in the form of selfishness and violence, but even more profoundly and perniciously in the divisions evident within each of us. One form this division takes is the classic distinction often made in the Western tradition between body and soul, or between body, mind, and spirit. On the surface, these divisions seem to make a lot of sense. All of us have bodily realities rooted in biological needs. We have to eat, sleep, and exercise; we have deep desires for physical intimacy; we are aware of our bodily limitations through fatigue, disease, or aging; at some point, we will die. At the same time, most of us recognize that humans are not governed by biological instincts or bodily passions alone. We have a capacity for rational thought. We can analyze the world in which we live, decode the mysterious forces of gravity, recognize patterns in nature, develop vaccinations against diseases, and plan for the future. Moreover, we also know that we are spiritual creatures. We experience the mysteries of love, joy, happiness, and hope; we have a deep awareness of moral order and justice; we sense a coherence to the world that defies rational explanation; we yearn for a relationship with God.

The Anabaptist-Mennonite understanding of the incarnation rejects the deep human tendency to pull apart these aspects of our humanity. Because God is present in all creation and because in Jesus, God and humanity become one, our biological, rational, and spiritual identities are grounded in the same life-giving source. Because every human being is a person of dignity—made in God's image, breathing the divine breath of life—our bodies can never be regarded as mere things. The incarnation invites us to live deeply in the reality that each of us is a unique child of God, a wondrously complex fusion of a living body, an active mind and a sensitive spirit, infinitely precious to God and to those around us.

In the Anabaptist-Mennonite tradition this understanding has led to the inescapable conviction that Christians can never willingly take the life of another human being, even if the nation—or one's natural instincts—justify such violence. In educational settings, this means that students are never merely bodies taking up seats in a classroom, or tuition-paying units that help the institution meet the budget, or athletes whose talents might bring glory to the school. Nor are they merely minds waiting to be filled or test-takers to be trained to pass the next set of standards. By the same token, they are also not merely spiritual beings to be instructed in right doctrine, souls to be saved, or psyches to be manipulated into a particular emotional state that we sometimes confuse with "being spiritual."

Educators in Mennonite schools will consciously treat each other and their students as whole persons. They will celebrate the body, but not worship it. They will celebrate the mind, though never as an end in itself. They will celebrate the spirit, knowing at the same time that God is revealed most fully to humans in the form of physical body. This unity of body, mind, and spirit reflects the character of the divine image within each of us.

5. Because of the Incarnation the World Matters

One final consequence of an Anabaptist-Mennonite theology of the incarnation is our relationship with the rest of the world. Christians whose lives have been transformed by Christ and the living presence of the Holy Spirit will inevitably want to share this good news with others. Those whose lives are shaped by the narrative of a God, active in history and calling creation back to its intended purpose, will want to participate with God in healing the world.

The Anabaptist-Mennonite tradition has not always been clear about its understanding of the world. On the one hand, following Jesus is an active and conscious choice to separate oneself from the illusions of selfishness and violence in order to become part of a "new creation" in Christ (2 Cor 5:17). The New Testament is full of passages that describe the Christian and the church as "called out" of the world; to "not be conformed" to the world (Rom 12:2); and even to despise the things of the world (Col 3). This view of the world as evil was confirmed for the early Anabaptists when they faced imprisonment, torture, and even death on account of their faith.

Yet there is also another theme in Scripture in which the people of God are called *out* of the world in order to be sent back *into* the world as agents of God's healing and hope. Throughout all of Scripture, God enters into the world's brokenness and pain in order to restore it to wholeness. The children of Israel had a special calling "to be a light to the nations" (Isa 49:6 NRSV; Acts 26:23). God loved the world so much that he was willing to send Jesus to bring the good news, even though this meant that Jesus would suffer and die on behalf of the world (John 3:16). Not surprisingly, the themes of reconciliation and healing were central to Jesus' entire ministry. Wherever he went, in every encounter, Jesus sought to bring together the divided, broken, or hurting. The most obvious instances were the miraculous acts of physical healing. But there are numerous examples of Jesus healing broken minds and spirits, offering new life to the spiritually dead, bringing together people at odds with each other, restoring dignity to those living in shame or at the margins of respectable society. This means that Christians who bear witness to an incarnational God will not retreat from the world in a quest for purity. Rather, in the course of their daily lives, they become the visible embodiment of God's presence in the world.

The Protestant tradition has strongly emphasized the power of the spoken word in missions. Sharing or preaching the gospel is a special vocation of the verbally gifted. This is not a small thing. But an even more powerful testimony of Christian witness is often evident in the surprising actions of believers who integrate the reconciling, healing presence of Christ into their daily lives—becoming the body of Christ made visible in the world.

This mission of reconciliation is expressed dramatically in Christ's death and resurrection. The Bible spares us few details about the reality of Christ's physical suffering, the emotional pain of betrayal, and the spiritual anguish of being separated from God. Yet the truly amazing part of the gospel story—the essence of the good news of the gospel—is not the crucifixion, but the *resurrection*. The physical body of Christ—beaten, crucified, speared, and left for dead—could not be contained in the tomb. The resurrection testifies to the fact that the God who created life is more powerful than the divisive forces of sin and death.

Education in Mennonite schools should prepare students for this calling to a life of ministry in the world: to heal the sick, to bind up the wounds of the oppressed, to stand alongside the poor and dispossessed, and to confront, as Jesus did, tyrants, bullies, and enemies with the good news of peace, reconciliation, and love.

Those who follow in the Anabaptist tradition will be fully engaged in the world—challenging, inviting, modeling, suffering, pouring themselves out for the world—so that the world might also participate in the joy of a reconciled life as God intended for all creation.

Conclusion

Our world is filled with broken, divided, lonely, and alienated people. In Jesus, God took on human form—the Word became flesh. The good news of the gospel is that Jesus has come to break down "dividing walls of hostility" (cf. Eph 2:14). Christians are called to bear witness to the incarnation. And in so doing, we are called to invite all those who are broken, divided, lonely, and alienated into the joy of new life, nourished by the vine of Christ, and bearing fruit of reconciliation and wholeness.

The consequences of this view of the gospel extend to all areas of life. But in Anabaptist-Mennonite schools they will be especially evident in the ethos of the school's culture, the style of classroom pedagogy, and the shared expectations regarding student outcomes.

To these themes we now turn.

Creating Communities of Learning:

The Ethos and Practices of an Anabaptist-Mennonite Pedagogy

"I was a pretty anxious person in high school," the college student told me. "Looking back now, I recognize it as one of the most difficult periods of my life."

My question had been open-ended but simple. I had asked her to recall some highlights of her time in Mennonite schools. Seventh and eighth grade had been manageable, she said. She had friends and kept up with her schoolwork. But she also struggled with anxiety. "Whatever I did or said always sounded stupid. I was very self-conscious about everything." The transition to high school only magnified her anxieties. One fall day in her ninth-grade year, things came to a head. A minor incident brought her to tears. Embarrassed to be seen crying, she impulsively left the classroom. Eventually she found refuge at the back of the school building and sat down, hidden behind some large shrubs, where she continued to cry quietly. Only a few minutes had passed when she saw two large feet under the shrubs and looked up to see "Grandpa" Troyer standing above her. Grandpa Troyer was a retired farmer who had served the school for years as a handyman and groundskeeper. He was a large, gentle man, who knew each of the students by name and greeted them warmly as they arrived each day. Now, without a word, he sat down near her. "Sometimes it's good to cry a little," he said. When her sobbing subsided, he asked her quietly, "Do you think you're ready to go back in?" She nodded. Grandpa Troyer helped her to her feet and walked her back to the classroom. When they arrived, he spoke a brief word to the teacher, and she settled into her desk to resume her studies.

"He recognized my need for space and silence," recalled the young woman. "It was exactly what I needed at that moment. And then he made it possible for me to become part of the community again."

It may seem odd to begin a chapter on Anabaptist-Mennonite pedagogy with a story about a high school groundskeeper. Grandpa Troyer was not a trained theologian; nor was he schooled in educational theory. Indeed, he was not even a classroom teacher. But the scene that transpired outside the school on that fall day offers an insight into how Mennonite schools, grounded in an incarnational theology, might think about pedagogy.

Pedagogy (from Greek, "to lead a child") is simply the conscious reflection on the nature of teaching. Pedagogy begins with the assumption that teaching is a skill that can be practiced, assessed, and improved. Classroom management, curricular planning, thoughtful assignments, techniques for engaging students, and assessment tools are all elements of successful pedagogy. But pedagogy from an Anabaptist-Mennonite perspective goes beyond technique alone. Pedagogy also includes the larger context within which education takes place: the unarticulated attitudes and assumptions that shape the feel of a classroom or school. Classroom pedagogy is often expressed as much in the gestures, habits, and character of a teacher as it is in formal strategies of teaching.

At its heart, Anabaptist-Mennonite pedagogy is about relationships.

Since the time of the ancient Greeks, teachers have tried to reflect carefully on the art of teaching, sorting out the many complex steps that unfold in the creative process of discovery and learning. Educational theorists have engaged in fierce debates on whether this discussion should focus primarily on the teacher or the student; whether pedagogy should concentrate on subject content or skills; whether the goal of education is conformity to social conventions or independent thinking; and whether teaching is a value-neutral or a consciously moral enterprise. And these themes barely scratch the surface. Anyone who has spent time reading the vast literature on pedagogy knows that a single chapter cannot do justice to all of these interesting and complex questions, especially in light of the fact that schools affiliated with the Mennonite Education Agency range from prekindergarten to seminary.

Thus the goal of this chapter is not to provide an overview of the literature of pedagogy or a comprehensive summary of the issues at stake. Rather, I want simply to highlight several key pedagogical themes consistent with a theology rooted in the incarnation and to propose a number of characteristics that I think should be evident in all teachers employed at a Mennonite school.

Because teaching never takes place in a vacuum, that conversation begins with a discussion of the ethos, or the *invisible curriculum*, of an Anabaptist-Mennonite school. Frequently the most powerful forces that shape our teaching are those that are least explicit—the unspoken assumptions woven into the institutional culture of our schools. Although it is appropriate for many of these assumptions to remain beneath the surface, administrators and teachers in healthy schools should not take them for granted. Since the invisible curriculum is the soil within which classroom pedagogy takes root, it needs to be carefully cultivated and tended.

The second half of the chapter offers specific suggestions regarding a classroom pedagogy shaped by Anabaptist-Mennonite perspectives. What are the habits, dispositions, or qualities that parents and students could expect to find in the classrooms and among the teachers of all MEA schools? The arguments put forth in this section may be rooted more firmly in ideals than in reality, and it is likely that not all readers will agree on these ideals. But I hope that the characteristics of good teaching suggested here serve as a frame of reference for ongoing and vigorous conversation among board members, administrators, teachers, parents, and congregations on the crucial question of pedagogy in the Anabaptist-Mennonite context.

Ethos: The Invisible Curriculum

It is easy for a teacher to think of the classroom as a kingdom unto itself. After all, the teacher shapes the curriculum, spends the most time with students, leads discussions, makes assignments, grades exams, and submits final evaluations. It is tempting to assume that questions of pedagogy begin and end within the confines of the classroom.

Yet however important the role of individual teachers—and they are exceedingly important!—what happens in the classroom always unfolds within a larger context. Long before individual teachers create a syllabus or meet their students for the first time, another curriculum—what might be called an "invisible curriculum"—is already in place, setting the tone and character for whatever happens in the classroom.

By its very nature, the invisible curriculum is never easy to define or assess, which makes it all the more powerful. Shaped by a long history of decisions, priorities, and patterns of relationships, the ethos of a school always has many complex, interrelated layers that cannot be fully captured in a marketing brochure or the text of a vision or mission statement. Though it is teachers who assign grades to students and administrators who tend to schedules and budgets, it is much more difficult to know who is in charge of the school's invisible curriculum. Yet every institution has a collective ethos—an overarching culture—that creates a shared environment and sets the tone for whatever happens within the classroom.

Some aspects of this ethos are fairly obvious. For example, does the school have a dress code? What are the policies regarding behavior? What courses are required of all students? What is the tone of assemblies and chapel? How are disciplinary procedures enforced? How does communication happen between administrators and teachers or between school and parents? Answers to these questions provide an important window into the school's ethos.

Frequently, however, the school's invisible curriculum is more subtle and difficult to pin down. What is the social "feel" of the school? Is student culture friendly or snobbish, open or cliquish? What are the attitudes of professors and students toward learning? Are they genuinely excited or merely putting in their time? Are expectations for students high or low? What sort of collaboration happens among teachers? What kind of relationships does the school have with supporting pastors or congregations? What is the status of athletics within the school? What is acceptable behavior among the fans who support the teams? All of these qualities shape the environment within which teaching and learning occurs.

Perhaps it is unreasonable to expect agreement on every aspect of the invisible curriculum in Mennonite schools. But as a starting point for the conversation, I suggest three characteristics—each of them emerging directly from a theology of the incarnation—that should be present in all Anabaptist-Mennonite communities of learning. Administrators interested in assessing the invisible curriculum of their schools could start by asking newcomers if they perceive these qualities to be evident in the established culture of their institution.

A Culture of Worship

In the first place, the invisible curriculum of Anabaptist-Mennonite schools should be shaped by a climate of worship. Initially it might sound strange to speak of worship in the context of pedagogy, especially in any school other than a seminary. After all, Mennonite schools are not churches, and they include students who may not embrace the Christian faith or share the stated values of Anabaptist-Mennonite belief and practice. Moreover, parents expect their children to learn about reading, writing, math, biology, sociology, and history at school—not spend the entire day in worship. It may be fine to have a thirty-minute chapel, a required Bible class or two, or even an occasional classroom prayer, but most of the time we do not think of educational institutions primarily as places of worship.

This skeptical response makes sense if, like many Christians, we think of worship primarily as something that happens for two hours on Sunday morning in a church building or in other conscious acts of prayer or piety. But if Anabaptist-Mennonite theology is truly incarnational, then our schools should resist the common temptation of dividing formal worship from daily life. Because God is the source of all creation and because each of us is made in God's image and breathes the breath of the divine Spirit, it is appropriate to frame *all* our work as an expression of worship.

Worship is not so much an action as a way of being, woven into the habits and consciousness of the entire community, that is continuously attentive to God's living presence in the world. Worship in the invisible curriculum finds expression not only in the formal gestures of prayer, songs, sermons, and retreats, but also in small things like the daily habits of silence, the memorization of Scripture, the repetition of the Lord's Prayer, or postings of wall mottos, icons, and Bible verses.

This attentiveness to the possibility of worship in everything we do can hold in check the impulse in our culture to think of education primarily as an intellectual enterprise. Education in the public school setting focuses on cognitive skills: becoming smarter, learning more information, and cultivating certain critical, technical, or analytical skills. Even Christian educators often frame their work around cognitive outcomes: to know more about the Bible, to learn doctrines of the faith, or to develop Christian arguments that can stand toe to toe against the atheists in our culture. Yet from the time of St. Augustine in the fourth and fifth centuries, Christians have also recognized that at a very deep level we are shaped by our hearts as much as our heads. Ultimately it is not cognitive thought that animates our passions but rather our desires, the stirrings of our hearts. And what we desire and love always has a target. So the question in educational settings is not, in the first instance, what we will *learn*, but what we will *love*. What will be the focus or the object of our affections?

Augustine also knew that the objects of our affections can be easily confused. Humans are inclined by sin to have "disordered desires." Scripture is filled with stories of God's people who went astray by worshipping the wrong things—false gods and idols. This is just as true today as it was then. We are constantly tempted to make the wrong things the highest objects of our desire. Thus, for example, without really intending to, parents can make children the objects of their worship. Students can make interactive technology, social status, or a promising career the primary focus of their desire. Schools can allow financial security, building projects, musical renown, or sports programs to become their gods.

The objects of our collective desire powerfully shape the invisible curriculum that sets the tone of classroom pedagogy. What would it look like for schools in the Anabaptist-Mennonite tradition to have as the primary object of their desire a hunger for God? Or to yearn for relationships grounded in dignity and trust? Or to pursue practices that treat God's creation with respect? Framing our priorities in this way creates a climate in which all of our activities are potential expressions of worship.

Shaping the ethos of an institution almost always starts with a conscious commitment on the part of the board and top administrators, and it usually finds expression in a number of formal and visible actions: explicit commitments in a mission or vision statement; focused themes at board or faculty retreats; and clear references to these priorities in contracts with teachers and staff, hallway conversations, editorials in the school newsletter, or in administrative updates in mailings to constituents. Intentional reflection on work as worship might also shape the topics addressed in chapel, teachers' meetings, or in-service retreats. The point in all of this is not to retreat into tired clichés (what is sometimes called "God Talk"), or to enforce obligatory prayer before every class, or to confuse references to God with a posture of worship. But joining daily practices with visual reminders and the communal rhythm of chapel or morning and evening prayers shape an ethos oriented to worship.

In so doing, we participate in a pedagogy of *rightly ordered desires*, which helps us to qualify our allegiance to other good things—sports, music, drama, academic achievements—and invites all members of the community to share in the Christian mystery of "praying without ceasing" (1 Thes 5:17).

Attentiveness to Tradition

Another significant element of the invisible curriculum—
the formative assumptions that shape a school's ethos and
pedagogy—are the stories that define a school's community. Schools, like families or nations, have a collective
identity that goes beyond colorful brochures, sparkling
new facilities, or the stump speeches of school administrators. That identity is formed, communicated to new
students, and passed along to successive generations in
the form of stories.

Stroll down the halls of almost any school building
and take note of what you see. The things that are visible
in public spaces say a great deal about the stories that
matter most to the institution: a school motto, student
artwork, photos from the past, a trophy case of athletic
achievements, the names of generous patrons.

The stories embodied in these visual markers affect
our pedagogy because what students learn is almost
always shaped by a deeper and larger tradition than what
is immediately evident in the classroom. The most basic
elements of that tradition in Mennonite schools have
come out of the biblical story—the ancient accounts of
God's mighty acts and outstretched arm in history that
culminate in the life, teaching, death, and resurrection of
Jesus, and continue to play themselves out in the daily
lives of Christians today. Even though these ancient stories may seem familiar to those who grew up in Christian homes, human beings are actually quite forgetful.
Indeed, the Old Testament is filled with admonitions to
create physical reminders of God's story as a public way
of marking memory and tradition. Piles of stones, carv-
ings on doorways, and even the mark of circumcision all
served as visible, tangible reminders to the children of
Israel that God had been at work in their lives, that they
stood in continuity with a story much deeper than the

present moment, and that they had an ongoing part to play in the story's unfolding.

Christians today are no different. We need regular reminders of the deeper stories and traditions that anchor us amid constant change and pressing challenges. By repeatedly telling the stories of Scripture, we ground ourselves within the larger story of God.

At the same time, our schools are also part of a more specific tradition within God's larger story. Recalling stories of faithfulness among Anabaptist or Mennonite men and women in our history as particular "incarnations" of God's presence in the world also shapes the ethos of our schools. Our schools should cultivate a living memory of the Anabaptist-Mennonite story, along with its deep roots in broader Christian history. We should tell stories of Anabaptist faithfulness amid persecution and suffering. We should remember their numerous migrations as pilgrims and strangers," grateful for the freedom to worship and work in peace but always ready to leave if the nation found their commitment to nonviolence too much of a threat to national security. There should be stories of gratitude for God's blessings, along with confessions of selfishness and greed. There should be stories of how the Anabaptist-Mennonite faith tradition has spilled out beyond the confines of culture and ethnicity to be embraced by other Christians around the world—so that the movement that started in Europe and thrived in North America now is growing most rapidly in the continents of Africa, Asia, Australia, and South America. There should be stories of God's grace and judgment, of faithfulness and failure, of community and conflict—all crucial threads woven into the larger fabric of the invisible curriculum.

An invisible curriculum attentive to tradition will also need to include the stories of one's own institution.

Why was the school formed? Who were the pioneers and heroes of faith associated with its early history? How has their vision been reshaped and transformed over the years? What were the moments of great conflict and uncertainty, of triumph and success? Each of us receives the past as a gift. So we must ask ourselves: What will be our contributions to the story? What gifts will we pass on to successive generations?

Telling the stories of one's own school is not just a matter of institutional pride, but also a way of giving concrete expression to a deeper sense of communal memory. Rooted in God's story and the Anabaptist-Mennonite tradition, and passed down from one generation to the next, stories are transformed and renewed by the telling.

Granted, telling stories of a particular faith tradition runs against the grain of modern culture, which prefers the general and generic over the particular. And focusing on these stories can seem exclusive to those who are not part of a Mennonite congregation. Yet as I have suggested earlier, particularity of identity is not a choice. Every school, like every congregation, will always have a set of convictions, stories, and boundaries that shape its theological identity. But if the particularity of identity is not a choice, you *can* choose the stories you tell about yourself. The highest expression of hospitality that a school can show to newcomers is to communicate, graciously and winsomely, the central themes of its tradition. Schools affiliated with MEA are, by definition, opting to associate themselves with the Anabaptist-Mennonite tradition. And the ethos of those schools should be such that testimonies of Christian faithfulness within the Anabaptist-Mennonite tradition can be told freely and confidently—not in a triumphalist tone, but with clarity and enthusiasm.

Like worship, recalling tradition-shaping stories requires attentiveness and thoughtful planning. Bible classes and chapel programs are two obvious settings for passing along these stories, along with rituals of welcome and departure, anniversaries that structure the rhythms of the school year, special occasions focused on the past, and events to honor alumni by inviting them to tell their own stories. But there are also ways of integrating this attentiveness to tradition into classroom settings as well. The themes of posters on bulletin boards, the selection of readings and research topics, or spontaneous sharing in classroom discussions all contribute to the overall atmosphere of the school.

What are the traditions that are woven into the ethos of your school? Be attentive to the stories you tell because they are shaping your pedagogy even if you are not aware of it.

Negotiating Community: Diversity, Conflict, and Reconciliation

A final component of the invisible curriculum—the shared context that shapes classroom pedagogy in Anabaptist-Mennonite schools—is the complex web of personalities, policies, memories, and relationships joining individual students, teachers, staff, and administrators into a learning community. Every school has a set of legal documents that constitute the institution as a corporation. Most schools also have handbooks that summarize the institution's mission, vision, and goals; define hiring practices; and set policies for staff. All schools have a set of buildings and grounds—a physical space—along with a board, an administrative team, faculty, and staff. All of these components are crucial elements of the school's identity. But what makes the school a living community is more than the sum of these parts.

Community is one of those words that is sure to turn up in every school's marketing literature and recruitment posters. Every school imagines itself to be a community.

Yet the actual reality of life together is never as tidy as the word suggests. In truth, the qualities that make for strong, healthy, dynamic communities are not simple to orchestrate or define. Community is lived and experienced, but it is never quite reducible to a formula.

In the context of a Christian school, community begins with a commitment to participate in a complex set of overlapping relationships, some of them formal (e.g., teacher contracts, syllabi, report cards), but many of them informal (e.g., hallway conversations with colleagues, board members raising money for a building project, a student seeking help on an assignment, an information technology person trying to fix your computer). These relationships are built slowly over time. They are deeply conditioned by past experiences and lingering memories, yet they are also always dynamic and open to change. Assumptions about the quality of all these relationships within a school—how individuals are treated, how conflict is resolved, how ready people are to collaborate—are crucial elements in the invisible curriculum.

Life in community would be easy if everyone had a similar history, shared the same tastes and values, had equal talents and aptitudes, and if nothing ever changed. But who would want to live in such a community? In reality, we find ourselves in relationships with people who are very different from ourselves. Indeed, most schools explicitly celebrate racial, cultural, economic, and religious diversity as something positive. Moreover, the context of our work is constantly changing, which requires communities to adapt and change in response. This means that healthy communities will always need to balance the inevitable diversity of individual differences and the constant reality of change with a deeper sense of coherence and a shared commitment to a larger whole. What holds it all together? What keeps communities united around a shared mission and purpose?

The standard response in the North American political context is the principle of individual rights and equality under the law. In a school setting, this means something like the equal treatment of all individuals according to the established policies of the institution. But even though clear policies are important for healthy relationships, a Christian understanding of community goes beyond the principles of rights and justice. Jesus made this point in the Sermon on the Mount (Matt 5-7) when he contrasted the legal principles of justice inherited from the Jewish tradition (e.g., "an eye for an eye and a tooth for a tooth") with the qualities of relationships that he envisioned in the new community he was initiating. Here relationships of love, mercy, generosity, and forgiveness trumped the fixed principles of giving each person their due.

A key image of community in the New Testament is that of the body—a living, breathing organism in which many different and diverse parts work together in the interests of the whole (1 Cor 12; Eph 4:11-16). It is precisely the weaker members of the body, Paul insists in 1 Corinthians 12, who are worthy of special attention (12:23). The ligaments or glue that holds this diversity together is not political correctness or slavish commitment to equality defined by a court of law. Rather, a Christian community is joined together by a shared commitment to Christ, in whom there is "neither Jew nor Greek, slave nor free, male nor female" (Gal 3:28) and by the common bond of the Holy Spirit.

To be sure, Mennonite schools are not the same as congregations. Students will inevitably have widely varying levels of commitment to the Christian faith; and none of us have been baptized into church membership in the schools for which we work. But administrators, teachers, and staff in Mennonite schools should be committed to living in Christian relationships with each other.

To acknowledge and celebrate this unity in Christ is not to negate or ignore differences. It suggests a shared commitment to look on each other first as children of God rather than as representatives of some sociological, cultural, or racial category. It assumes that in our relationships with each other—our work, recreation, worship, singing, and sharing—we treat each other compassionately and as whole people, made in the image of God. This means that we will treat everyone we encounter with dignity—not as bodies or as objects, but as bearers of the image of God and carriers of the divine breath. It means that Mennonite schools will be especially attentive to individuals and groups who feel marginalized. Mennonite schools will work against patterns of patriarchy that grant men special privileges and against the deep structures of racism that secure white privilege, even though these dynamics are often invisible.

The ethos of community is also deeply shaped by how community members resolve conflicts. Disruptions to community harmony are all around us. Diversity, change, and disequilibrium are inevitable. In schools, this can take many forms: the emergence of doctrinal differences within supporting congregations; a fifteen-year-old student who becomes pregnant; an influx of students who do not speak English as a first language; teachers who disagree about disciplinary approaches; administrators who seem to favor one department over another; carefully laid budgetary plans disrupted by low enrollment; a beloved teacher who resigns unexpectedly; a group of students arrested for underage drinking; a gifted student who hacks into the computerized grading system; a seemingly harmless prank that sets off the fire alarm and sprinkler system, causing thousands of dollars worth of damage. How board, administrators, teachers, and staff respond to the realities of diversity and conflict is crucial to the ethos of the school. It shapes an important part of the invisible curriculum.

Healthy communities are filled with people who honestly speak their minds and have the courage to act with clarity and decisiveness. The Anabaptist martyrs were no pushovers. At the same time, however, the Anabaptist-Mennonite tradition's commitment to nonviolence also extends to relationships. It is possible to testify to our understandings of truth in ways that do not demean or diminish the dignity of the other. In Matthew 18, Jesus outlines a clear process for discipline that is restorative. Differences are openly acknowledged, but always in a spirit of love, recognizing the possibility that one's own perception is faulty, and with the goal of restoring relationships (Gal 6:1-2).

It is not always easy to get this right. A commitment to nurturing healthy communities requires risk-taking and vulnerability, along with a willingness to ask for and to receive forgiveness. Attitudes of empathy and compassion are learned behaviors. They need to be taught, modeled, reinforced, and practiced. Ultimately, a commitment to community is a visible expression of God's incarnated presence breaking into a broken world. To participate in community is to share in the redemption of creation.

The invisible curriculum is not easy to talk about since it is woven so deeply into the rhythms of daily life. Yet a *posture of worship*, attentiveness to *tradition*, and *relationships of healthy community* profoundly shape the teaching and learning that happens in our schools.

What would an institutional audit of your invisible curriculum reveal?

Pedagogical Practices: Embodying Virtue in the Classroom

If you ever want to start a lively conversation at a dinner party, ask those present to recall their favorite teacher and to share a story or two that captures the essence of what made that teacher so special. Everyone will have something to share. And it is likely that the memories of favorite teachers will have some commonalities, regardless of whether the stories come from elementary school, high school, or college.

For millennia, Greek philosophers, Jewish rabbis, and ordinary people have debated the characteristics of great teachers. That debate is ongoing. Educational theorists have still not established complete consensus on what those qualities might be, nor have they settled the question as to whether these qualities can be learned or whether they are simply intrinsic to a great teacher's personality. Yet reflecting on memorable teachers opens up an important conversation about the nature of good pedagogical practices in an Anabaptist-Mennonite educational context.

In what follows I will not be addressing the current controversies over specific classroom methodologies—for example, the ongoing debates about how best to teach reading or the relative merits of inductive versus deductive approaches to math education. These are surely important conversations, but our goal is to focus instead on the qualities of teaching, consistent with Anabaptist-Mennonite convictions, that might apply to a wide range of educational settings.

These qualities can be learned. They are not simply divine gifts bestowed on a lucky few, while the rest of us are consigned to pedagogical mediocrity. Yet the characteristics of good teachers are best understood as dispositions rather than methodologies or techniques.

A disposition is a cultivated habit: a practiced attentiveness to a way of living repeated so often that the distinction between habit and conscious action becomes blurred. Dispositions are about the quality of character that inclines (or "disposes") us to act in a particular way. Cultivating dispositions requires intentionality and practice. Dispositions are formed slowly over time, and they are practiced in the context of a larger community of people who are also committed to nurturing those same qualities in their own lives until they eventually become habits that feel natural or are second nature.

Think of pedagogical dispositions as analogous to the skills of a gifted athlete. Athletic excellence always begins at a basic level: we watch others play a sport well and are inspired to start practicing ourselves. If we want to become good at a sport, we will need to engage in focused and disciplined training, both on our own and in the hands of gifted coaches. We submit to hours of practice, some of which involve repetitive exercises that do not necessarily come naturally to us. And we do all of this in the company of others who are also committed to becoming excellent. Along the way, we might study the history of our sport, spend hours reading about the truly great players, and debate with our colleagues about the fine details of the game. And we might study a playbook or carefully observe from the sidelines. But mostly we learn by playing the sport. The great players are always keenly attentive to the dynamics of their sport, learning as they go, constantly asking how they might do it better. If we stick with the training regimen and compete regularly, we slowly recognize that what seemed impossible when we first started now seems almost automatic. Certain moves, reactions, or gestures begin to feel natural—as if we have been doing them all our lives.

The dispositions that make for pedagogical excellence in Mennonite schools are cultivated in a similar way. The difference between great teachers and mediocre teachers is less a question of sheer giftedness than it is a willingness to engage consciously in the habits and practices that make for great teaching. Certainly not every individual will exhibit all of the qualities of a great teacher in equal measure. But it is reasonable to expect all teachers to be committed to pedagogical excellence and to hold them accountable for their progress toward that goal.

The list of specific pedagogical dispositions that I identify below is not exhaustive. Nor are these characteristics found exclusively among teachers in Mennonite schools. But these follow naturally from a theology rooted in the incarnation and are consistent with an invisible curriculum committed to worship, tradition, and community.

As teachers model these dispositions in their daily encounters with students, they not only create a context for learning the subject matter at hand, they also invite students to nurture similar dispositions, which will enhance their learning for the rest of their lives.

1. Curiosity: Humility Seeking Understanding

Teachers in Anabaptist-Mennonite schools will model a pedagogy of curiosity. Why is the sky blue? Why do birds sing? What happens when water freezes? These questions may seem obvious and basic, and one certainly does not need to be at a Christian school to find the answers to them. But the curiosity that gives rise to these and a thousand other questions is not to be taken for granted. A disposition of curiosity implies an awareness of the breadth and depth of our ignorance as well as an attitude of wonder toward creation and a hunger to learn more. A curious teacher recognizes the complexity of the world in all its dimensions—natural, social, and spiritual—and is not afraid to acknowledge the limits of knowledge, since this is only a prelude to deeper understanding.

One could look at education primarily as a transfer of information from teacher or textbook to student or as a set of specific skills taught in a clearly prescribed fashion. But genuine curiosity assumes that all of us—teacher and students alike—are engaged in an ongoing process of inquiry. To be sure, teachers have more training and knowledge than students, and they have a larger number of resources at their disposal. But no matter how often a teacher covers the material in a given class, there is always more to be discovered. Moreover, there is always the added dimension of engaging familiar material with a new combination of students, who bring fresh experiences and perspectives to the conversation.

A pedagogy of curiosity models Christian humility by making it clear that humans have not yet plumbed the full depth of our wondrously complex universe. In this sense, curiosity honors the incarnation. It recognizes that God is always latent in creation, waiting to be revealed. But this revelation is never complete or fully within our grasp. Our knowledge is always finite, always limited. Behind every answer are still more questions. In the richness of God's creation, there is always more to be learned.

A pedagogy of curiosity recognizes that learning how to ask good questions may be as important a measure of educational success as possessing a lot of right answers. This should not be confused with a disdain for factual information or a relativist notion that all answers are more-or-less equally correct. In my own discipline of history, taking the time to study basic facts is a crucial first step in learning to think like a historian. Inquiry into the truth directs us toward deeper understanding of the way things really are. But simply lining up facts correctly or memorizing information is not ultimately the goal of Christian education. In our information-rich age, students are always only a few keystrokes away from finding basic factual information on Google or Wikipedia. More challenging, and infinitely more interesting, is an ability to ask questions that probe beneath the factual information to the intricacies and interconnections that hold together the wonder of life.

2. Reason: Celebrate the Gift of the Mind

Our sense of curiosity and hunger for answers find direction and discipline in the God-given gift of reason. A disposition to cultivate the rational qualities of our mind recognizes the hand of God behind the order of creation, an order sometimes hidden from sight, but present nonetheless for those willing to patiently pursue it. Reason probes beneath the apparent chaos of our daily life to seek out patterns of interconnection that often hide below the surface. God has given us minds to explore the wonders of creation: to probe the far reaches of outer space, to investigate the complex world of a single cell, to inquire into the mysteries of molecular interactions, to discern the wondrous patterns of mathematics, to explore the miracle of minds and brains, to wrestle with the deep questions of theology. We sometimes think of reason as the special focus of the hard sciences—math, physics, biology, or chemistry. Yet reason is relevant to all disciplines, including biblical studies and Christian ethics. Using evidence and logic, reason leads us to a deeper understanding of the world.

Our human impulse is to act according to our instincts and passions. Yet we also have a capacity for abstract and reflective thought. Thanks to the gift of reason, we can step outside ourselves and see ourselves as actors, capable of meaningful choices, based on a clear sense of options. The Anabaptist-Mennonite tradition has always recognized that faith is not only a gift, but also a choice. By honoring the voluntary nature of our decision to follow Christ, we affirm reason as a divine gift.

Like curiosity, reason is never an end in itself. In the Western tradition it is easy to make an idol of reason, as if it were the only quality necessary for an educated person. Students of the natural sciences, guided only by reason, can reduce humans to their genetic code or body chemistry, just as social scientists can reduce humans to little more than profit seekers, statistical collectives, or maximizers of self-interest. Christian educators need to be attentive to the arrogance lurking within the gift of reason—that persistent human impulse to worship ourselves rather than the Creator.

Yet reason is clearly a gift of God. Properly applied, it enables teachers and students to explore the mysteries of creation and, in the process, to become medical researchers, engineers, development workers, and diplomats prepared to participate in the restoration of God's creation to its intended purpose.

Teachers who cultivate a disposition of reason will model careful thinking. They will help students recognize the structure of coherent arguments; they will refuse to be satisfied with answers that do not make sense or that insist on ignoring what the evidence suggests. No question—including questions of Christian faith and practice—should be off-limits in a Mennonite school.

A Mennonite pedagogy should model the gift of reason.

3. Joy: Education Is Not Drudgery

In his autobiography, *Surprised by Joy*, C. S. Lewis recalls a moment early in his life when he experienced a flash of sheer joy.[14] As he describes that moment—crucial to his decision to become a Christian—Lewis recognizes that this experience of sudden and unexpected exhilaration was accompanied by an awareness of a deep coherence to the entire universe, a certainty that the world was held together in a remarkable and beautiful way.

Shaped by a theology of the incarnation, Mennonite educators will be constantly alert to such moments of joy in their classrooms. They will cultivate a disposition open to the "aha!" thrill of discovery and the delight that comes when we are surprised to find beauty in unexpected places.

So often the general attitude toward education is one of obligation and dreary labor. Administrators sometimes joke about the prison-like nature of school. Teachers occasionally act as if school is a grind that must be endured while waiting for real pleasures on weekends and summer vacations. College students sometimes spend hours playing video games in an effort to avoid their schoolwork.

Clearly, some aspects of teaching and learning require the discipline of hard work. Sometimes rote memorization is simply the best way to integrate information into our brains. At times, teachers need to force themselves to grade essays or to complete assignments when they would rather do something else. But in the larger picture, teaching and learning should be a joyful enterprise. This is a task blessed with the pleasure of relationships and punctuated with the sudden recognition of patterns of human thought and behavior or connections in the natural world that God has laid out from the beginning. Learning is boring only when we pursue it in isolation or when we do not see any connections with the broader world. It is joyful when we have a sense that a mystery is being revealed through our interaction together.

Teachers and students can experience joy in many settings: in learning to decode the meaning of texts, in expressing thoughts in writing, in painting a picture, or practicing music. We can also experience joy in witnessing the accomplishments of others: the wonder of hearing a classmate perform a Mozart sonata on the piano, celebrating a friend's poem that perfectly expresses our sentiments, seeing a mathematical proof laid out in simple and elegant form, resolving a technical problem with a creative application of computer code. Behind all of this is a sense of deep joy in the recognition of God's presence in the world in such varied and wonderful forms.

To cultivate a disposition of joy in the classroom is not to be naive about the reality of suffering in the world or blind to the pain of others. We should work hard to understand the nature of the world's brokenness. We should struggle against injustice, greed, and violence in their many forms. But a pedagogy of joy calls us to engage that struggle recognizing that we are participating in something bigger than our puny efforts and that success or failure is ultimately not in our hands. Joy is not so much an emotion of happiness as it is an expression of eschatological hope. Joy accompanies our moment of recognition that God is ultimately in control of the world. In letting go, in yielding to God our own efforts to impose order on the world, we experience joy.

Because creation is latent with God's revelation, Anabaptist-Mennonite educators will engage in their work with joy.

4. Patience: "If You Knew It All You Would Not Need to Be Here"

A Mennonite pedagogy informed by the incarnation will cultivate a disposition of patience. We live in an instant culture. Our society is dedicated to speed. We have been conditioned to expect computers to operate instantaneously—at "twitch speed"—so that a delay of more than a millisecond generates a burst of impatience within us. Cell phones and Wi-Fi connect us to a vast network of instant communication and provide immediate access to information. Politicians must produce results in two- or four-year election cycles. Our food industry has been reconfigured around the promise of convenience and speed; we do not think twice about the merits of fast food or the benefits of instant potatoes, microwave popcorn, prepackaged cookie dough, or boneless chicken. We seem to have an insatiable appetite for get-rich-quick schemes, instant diets, or books promising to transform us overnight.

The educational system is not immune to this impulse toward greater efficiencies and faster results. Parents press hard to get their children enrolled in advanced courses. High schools are under increasing pressure to grant college credit. Distance learning courses, available around the clock, promise to offer an education without any disruption to your job or any other commitments. Students can instantly produce papers by downloading them directly from the Internet. And a whole host of companies will send you an advanced degree immediately—without any requirements at all—if you are willing to pony up the cash.

In such a context, a pedagogy of patience is truly countercultural. Anyone who has worked with children or young adults recognizes that learning happens in many different ways and at many different speeds. At times it may appear as if no learning is happening at all. A Christian educator is like a good farmer, who tends to all the details that go into raising an abundant crop as the ground is prepared, seeded, fertilized, and watered. But patience is also crucial. Few seeds grow instantaneously, and a farmer cannot compel a single seed to grow simply by creating all the right conditions.

Moreover, students differ enormously in their personalities, interests, and learning styles. Teachers tend to focus their primary energies on students who learn quickly. The bigger challenge for educators, however, is how to reach out effectively to students who do not respond to traditional approaches. This requires attentiveness, creativity, and patience. Even students who are able to quickly master factual content or concepts are almost certainly going to take much longer to show progress in areas that matter most—the integration of that material into larger patterns of meaning, for example, or a genuinely creative engagement with the reading material, or growth in Christian virtue.

All of these qualities take a great deal of time to learn, and sometimes for long stretches, evidence of growth is not easy to recognize. Anyone who has tried to learn a new language knows that growth toward mastery of a another language is always incremental—often almost indiscernible—until one day you are surprised to realize that you are communicating at a level that once did not seem possible. I have been teaching long enough to refrain from making firm judgments about the future of students who seemed distracted or unengaged in their early years of college. Over the years I have witnessed many such students who have gone on to become highly successful voluntary service workers, pastors, entrepreneurs, and community leaders.

Although it is always tempting to blame students for their short attention spans, Christian educators should regard their students with the same attitude that God has shown us. The God revealed in the incarnation is, above all, patient and persistent. Restoring creation to its intended purpose takes a long time. Patience requires a practiced habit of what the early Anabaptists called *Gelassenheit* (German for "yieldedness"). *Gelassenheit* is a conscious relinquishing of our temptation to take charge, to force the issue, to press ahead, to fix the problem. It is a deliberate, practiced effort to look at the world through the eyes of God, against an eschatological horizon. *Gelassenheit* calls us to engaged, focused work while also recognizing that the fruit will ripen in God's own time.

Even though our cultural obsession with speed tempts us to look for shortcuts and quick solutions, educators in

Mennonite schools will be characterized by a posture of patience. They know that the things that matter most in life—like teaching children, developing committed relationships, building a community—require time, consistency, discipline, attentiveness, and patience.

5. Love: Created in the Image of God

In 1769, a Mennonite teacher at a small country school in Skippack, Pennsylvania, not far from Philadelphia, published the first book on pedagogy to appear in colonial America. In contrast to the standard pedagogical assumptions of the day, Christopher Dock rejected harsh disciplinary methods in his *Schul-Ordnung* (*School Management*), arguing that students responded best to a gentle approach based on persuasion and peer pressure, with a clear rationale for all forms of discipline.[15] Dock described numerous specific practices that contributed to his widely-recognized success as a teacher. Students especially prized, for example, his individualized gifts of artfully-decorated mottos (*Fraktur*) acknowledging their success. Students treasured these *Fraktur* so much that several dozen have survived to this day. But the main thrust of Dock's book focused on the significance of the relationship between teacher and student, a relationship rooted in mutual respect, trust and love.

Every afternoon, before returning home, Dock made it a practice to pray for each of his students. One morning in the winter of 1771, however, when students arrived at the Skippack schoolhouse they discovered their beloved teacher was dead. Dock had died on his knees the previous day, praying for his students.

Christopher Dock recognized that the relationship between a teacher and student forms the heart of pedagogy. One recurring theme in Dock's reflections on the role of a teacher, particularly in his chapters on classroom management, was his evident affection for each student

as a unique individual. Indeed, infusing all of his pedagogical wisdom was an awareness that teaching was an
expression of Christian love.

Dock did not describe this love primarily in emotional
terms. Instead he summarized it in a set of practices that
characterized all of his interactions with students. It
began with points as mundane as clarity about expectations. No rule existed without an explanation, which
Dock was sure to repeat even as he meted out some form
of discipline on students who had violated the classroom code. Dock expressed appreciation in public and
private for the specific ways each individual student had
contributed to the larger goals of the classroom. Dock
believed in a structured classroom—he thought long
and hard about how best to respond to students who
spoke out of turn, distracted their neighbors, failed to
complete assignments, or used inappropriate language.
At the same time, his specific suggestions for how to
resolve these classroom challenges always acknowledged the need for flexibility and exceptions, depending
on the circumstances.

Included in Dock's curriculum was a deep appreciation for the natural world. Love of God and love for each
other were closely linked with a love for God's creation—
which he evoked in the study of plants and animals, an
attentiveness to the changing seasons, and an appreciation for the starry heavens.

Above all, Dock was committed to making his classroom a community of learning in which the presence of
God was evident in everything he did. Respect for each
other, for nature, for parents and church all began with a
healthy understanding of a human's relationship to God.
As the psalmist writes, "The fear of the Lord is the beginning of wisdom" (Ps 111:10).

Although circumstances and cultural contexts have

changed since Christopher Dock published his *Schul-Ordnung*, the larger themes of his pedagogy continue to pose an inspiring challenge to educators in Mennonite schools today:

- a focus on relationships with students that is grounded in God's free, gracious love for us;
- an attentiveness to the individual qualities of each student, seeking the best for each pupil;
- modeling relationships of respect, trust, and mutuality;
- establishing a culture of peace, in which students are trained to hold firm and to have a clarity of conviction, even as they practice the spiritual fruit of "love, joy, peace, patience, kindness, goodness, faithfulness, gentleness and self-control" (Gal 5:22-23);
- daily prayer, even—perhaps especially—for those students who seem recalcitrant to the best pedagogical methods.

For educators in the Anabaptist-Mennonite tradition, a pedagogy rooted in the incarnation begins with the recognition that our students are not adversaries or enemies; nor are they blank slates, vessels to be filled, or putty in our hands. They are human beings, made in the image of God and with whom we have been entrusted to enter into a relationship. The apostle Paul summarizes it best in his letter to the church at Corinth:

> If I speak in the tongues of men and of angels, but have not love, I am only a resounding gong or a clanging cymbal. If I have the gift of prophecy and can fathom all mysteries and all knowledge, and if I have a faith that can move mountains, but have not love, I am nothing. If I give all I possess to the poor and surrender my body to the flames, but have not love, I gain nothing.

Love is patient, love is kind. It does not envy, it does not boast, it is not proud. It is not rude, it is not self-seeking, it is not easily angered, it keeps no record of wrongs. Love does not delight in evil but rejoices with the truth. It always protects, always trusts, always hopes, always perseveres.

Love never fails. . . . Now we see but a poor reflection [as in a mirror]; then we shall see face to face. Now I know in part; then I shall know fully, even as I am fully known.

And now these three remain: faith, hope and love. But the greatest of these is love. (1 Cor 13:1-8, 12-13)

Conclusion

Though different, all of these pedagogical dispositions—curiosity, reason, joy, patience, and love—express a similar goal. They all describe how the Word becomes flesh in educational settings—how the Spirit of God is made visible in this world of time and space. As educators, we bear witness to the wonder of the incarnation in our lesson plans and in our instruction, but especially in our modeling. By cheering, nudging, and encouraging, we nurture habits of attentiveness to the Spirit of God as that Spirit is revealed in relationships and in creation.

Classroom pedagogy in an Anabaptist-Mennonite mode is shaped by a larger schoolwide commitment to look upon the collective task through the lens of worship, shaped by a shared tradition and by the practices of a healthy, living community. It is embodied tangibly in the classroom by teachers committed to a pedagogy of curiosity, reason, joy, patience, and love. These qualities are not a formula or technique; but they are also not mysterious. They will always find expression in specific interactions, in daily practices, and in the concrete realities of life together.

All of this brings us back to Grandpa Troyer. The student with whom I spoke had dozens of memories from her time at a Mennonite school. She learned a great deal about biology, math, history, and English. She enjoyed her Bible classes and grew in her Christian faith. She made many good friends, played in sports, and was a gifted musician. But it was no accident that when I asked her to summarize what Christian education meant for her, the first story that came to mind was the vivid memory of Grandpa Troyer putting his Christian commitment into practice.

What happened that afternoon was one instance of the invisible curriculum being enacted. Those qualities will take on many different expressions, often informal and unplanned. But a school shaped by incarnational theology will bear witness to a God at work in restoring wholeness and harmony to a broken world.

Outcomes of a Mennonite Education:
Taste and See

One summer when our children were still at home, our family vacationed in the Western states, visiting numerous national parks and taking in beautiful and amazing sights. One of our most stunning and impressive memories came when we finally reached the Pacific Northwest. In southern Oregon and northern California we walked through the misty forests of the giant redwoods, looming high over the Pacific Ocean. Then we traveled southeast to visit Sequoia National Park. In rapt silence, dwarfed by the towering sequoias, we looked up in awe. Some of the trees, already ancient at the time of Christ, were more than 300 feet high and measured 60 feet in diameter. Through the centuries they have survived earthquakes, forest fires, and the spread of human civilization. Each year their massive trunks steadily add one more tiny ring of growth.

Not long after that experience, we visited a former student who was now working for the National Parks Service. As he described his work, he mentioned that one summer he had spent several months planting sequoias— digging holes for tiny seedlings, barely more than sticks, in the hope that they would take root.

Those images—of the ancient, towering mature trees

and the simple repeated act of planting a tiny sequoia sprig—have stayed with me ever since.

What a remarkable act of faith it is to plant a tree, knowing that it will likely be decades, perhaps even centuries, before that seedling will mature into a fully grown oak or a massive sequoia. Yet that is the hope to which all Christian educators are called. When we meet students for the first time, we agree to participate in small gestures of planting, watering, pruning, or nurturing. We do so as an expression of hope that at some point in the future— perhaps long after our direct contact with these students has ended—this time together will matter in ways that we can scarcely imagine.

A commitment to Christian education, like the radical gesture of planting a sequoia, reflects a long view of history. Through the decades the field of education has been extremely susceptible to a host of new theories, paradigm shifts, and alternative models of instruction, usually accompanied by a cluster of buzzwords, innovative technologies, massive infusions of money, and overheated promises about the likely outcomes. Anyone involved with formal education today has experienced the pressure to translate all of these resources into measurable outcomes.

Yet if standard measurements of educational success are to be trusted, little evidence suggests that any of these approaches has provided a breakthrough solution. According to the National Assessment of Educational Progress, average reading and math scores for high school seniors in the U.S. have remained essentially unchanged from the early 1970s to 2010 even as student-teacher ratios declined, teachers' salaries increased, and overall spending on education rose by 40 percent.[16] At the same time, numerous reports have suggested that American elementary and high school students continue to lag behind their counterparts in many other parts of the world in academic preparation.

Despite decades of anxious public hand-wringing, there is still little agreement on even the most basic questions of assessment. By what criteria should we measure educational success? Can true educational success even be quantified? If so, are underperforming students the victims of an inept educational system? Or is the real problem linked to some combination of larger social failures, such as urban poverty, family instability, the pervasive influence of electronic entertainment, misguided priorities of teachers unions, or underfunded schools?

These questions are relevant for church-related schools as well, along with the added dimension of the faith-based convictions and practices that we assume should be evident among students attending Mennonite schools. Here, as with the public school debate, the questions can easily overwhelm the answers. Exactly what do parents and congregations expect from Mennonite schools? Should the anticipated outcomes of students in MEA-affiliated schools be quantifiable in standardized forms of assessment, or should schools focus instead on the unique needs and abilities of each individual student? Are the qualities of a faith-based education even susceptible to quantifiable measurement? What is the place of grades and competition at a Mennonite school? Are there any outcomes that might be expected among all students across the full range of schools affiliated with MEA?

The Challenges of Assessment

One way to plunge into the welter of these difficult questions is to affirm from the outset that Mennonite schools should be committed to meeting or surpassing all baseline academic standards that one might expect to find in a well-run public school or college. Students who attend Mennonite schools also live in a larger culture in which they will need to function as productive citizens. Graduates of MEA-affiliated schools should be able to move into a complex economy and succeed in a wide variety of work settings. The appeal to a faith-based education should never serve as an excuse for low academic standards or inept teachers.

To do this, Mennonite schools need to provide their students with competent instruction in all of the standard subject areas. Are children learning to read? Can they negotiate basic mathematics? Can they write complete sentences? Do students have a sense of historical chronology and causal relationships? These basic skills associated with education at all the various levels are generally the easiest to define, quantify, and assess with standardized tests. And there may be very good reasons for Mennonite schools to include such tests in the curriculum.

At the same time, however, even though high-level competency in teaching is absolutely crucial, and even though standardized tests may provide some general baseline for assessment, Mennonite schools should never reduce their expectations for learning outcomes to these measures alone. In light of a theological commitment to a faith embodied in daily life and a pedagogical commitment to cultivating dispositions like curiosity, reason, joy, patience, and love, the educational standards in a Mennonite school will need to exceed mere competency in standard skill and content areas. Here, standardized tests are probably not the best method for assessing these qualities.

Consider the example of parenting. Any parent knows how much of that role is bound up with a host of small but important tasks: preparing meals, doing the laundry, buying groceries, paying bills, transporting children, making appointments. But if you ask a parent what it *means* to be parent, they would never reduce that role to these discrete tasks. The things that matter most about parenting cannot be so easily quantified. If a child asks a parent, "How much do you love me?" it is unlikely that the parent will respond with a number on a scale from one to a hundred. Instead, the parent turns poetic: "I love you as high as the sky" or "I love you as much as the water in all the oceans." In a similar way, a monk could give you a list of spiritual disciplines and how many hours a day he practices them, but this in itself would not likely be an accurate measure of his virtue or spiritual maturity.

Tests are good at measuring cognitive skills. But a Mennonite high school is not fulfilling its role if it graduates an entire class of National Merit finalists but has no idea if those students are more compassionate, have a deeper understanding of Scripture, have gained more insight into their role within a community, are able to see connections between their faith and their moral choices, or are more responsible stewards of creation. These outcomes, unfortunately, cannot be easily reduced to quantifiable measures. But if qualities like character, compassion and virtue matter, we should build them into the curriculum even if they are not easily measured by standardized tests.

A culture of test taking also evaluates students in relation to some absolute standard, which can minimize the unique gifts and needs of individual students. Thus a bright student who has simply attended class might score very high, whereas a student who is just beginning to understand the material and is rapidly moving toward deeper insights still remains below average. Our standard system of assigning grades does not account for the enormous variety in individual learning styles, level of individual effort, or willingness to take risks. Nor does it tell a teacher about differences in cultural background, the emotional well-being of the student, or the spiritual struggles that a student might be going through.

Pressures in our culture to compare test scores—and in so doing, to equate IQ or the outcome of state standards test or a college entrance exam score with the value of a person—are subtle but pervasive. From a Christian perspective the intellectual aptitude of an individual student should never be associated with a test score or some externally based measure of academic success. To the contrary, Mennonite schools should be especially attentive to the profound differences that exist among individual students in the same grade or age group. Our classrooms have students with wide variations in the level of support they receive from home, in language background, and in developmental pacing. Moreover, students inevitably reflect a variety of learning styles, which calls for great sensitivity and flexibility in pedagogical approaches. Since no single teaching style is likely to captivate the imagination or call forth the gifts of every student in the class, teachers must include variety in their assignments, collaborate frequently with other teachers, and demonstrate flexibility and sensitivity in their assessment methods.

Church-based schools and teachers should be held accountable to standards. But teachers in the Anabaptist-Mennonite tradition should be wary lest they reduce classroom goals to measurable results. They should be attentive to individual differences. And they should focus on outcomes that go beyond competency in content and skills alone.

Goals of an Anabaptist-Mennonite Education

This chapter proposes six goals of church-based education, each focused on one human sense. If the Word is to become flesh, then Christian education in an Anabaptist-Mennonite context should be embodied in visible ways. Although these outcomes are not easily assessed in quantifiable terms, the six goals I propose here suggest several key aspects of what it means to participate in the body of Christ as a witness to the wholeness and unity that God intends for all humanity and for all creation itself.

1. *Gifts of Sight and Perception: Seeing Details in a Larger Context*

When I was younger, I loved to read mystery novels of all sorts. But my clear favorites for a time were the stories of Sherlock Holmes. In addition to the eccentric characters and complex plot, I always looked forward to the moment in the novel when Sherlock would turn to his partner and say, "It's all very elementary, Watson!" Then Sherlock would proceed to explain the resolution to the mystery. Starting with one impossibly tiny detail—the pattern of dust on the hem of a woman's skirt or the smell of a particular brand of pipe tobacco—Holmes would unravel the mystery, so that by the end of his explanation it all seemed crystal clear. Once, when Watson pressed him on his uncanny ability to resolve the most tangled mystery, Holmes replied, "Most people only look at the world; but I *see* the world."

That distinction between "looking" and "seeing" may sound a bit presumptuous, but Sherlock Holmes had a point. Much of the time, most of us are content to simply go through life while barely noticing the world around us. But there also are key moments when we suddenly recognize a deeper dimension of reality—when we, like Holmes, no longer simply glance at the mundane details of our surroundings but become keenly aware of the profound interconnectedness of life, the intricate web of patterns and relationships that weaves a particular fact into a much bigger pattern of meaning.

One gift of modern life is the astonishing amount of information now at our fingertips. Thanks to the Internet, virtually anyone can have instant access to vast libraries of knowledge. This democratization of information is a remarkable achievement, a huge shift from earlier eras where information of all sorts was restricted to a privileged elite. Unfortunately, however, having access to an infinite amount of random information does not resolve life's deep questions. If education were primarily about gaining access to information, it would be much more efficient simply to teach every child how to use a search engine and set them loose on the Internet. Surfing the Internet allows us to look at lots of things, but it does not give us the capacity to truly "see" the world, to recognize how a specific detail fits within a larger pattern of meaning.

In the thirteenth century, the medieval theologian Thomas Aquinas tried to summarize all human knowledge in one of the Western world's first encyclopedias, which he called the *Summa theologica*. But unlike modern encyclopedias, whose topics are juxtaposed randomly by alphabet, Aquinas insisted that nothing could be truly known apart from its relationship to everything else; ultimately, all knowledge points to God, Creator of the world. So he organized the *Summa* as an intricately interconnected description of the created world, any single part of which could be traced back to God.

Medieval approaches to education have since fallen out of favor, especially in the aftermath of the Enlightenment, which insisted that facts can be separated from values, and that science is objective while ethics and theology are subjective. But an Anabaptist-Mennonite education, rooted in a view of the incarnation in which Christ is the "firstborn of all of creation" (Col 1:15) and the source of all order, will challenge this artificial separation of facts from the larger meaning.

Thus, one goal for students in all Mennonite schools should be steady growth in their vision or perception— a deepening ability not just to absorb the factual details of a subject, but also to see these details within a larger context of meaning and significance.

This can happen at many levels and in many subject areas. In the discipline of history, it begins by taking traditional approaches to the subject seriously. Students interested in the American Civil War, for example, cannot fully understand the meaning of those events without having some understanding of the contested history of slavery, the economic interests that divided the northern states from the southern states, or the long political debate about federalism versus states' rights. In a similar way, a chemistry student in a Mennonite school should be able to describe the molecular structure of water as a chemical compound formed by two parts hydrogen and one part oxygen (H_2O); they should have some understanding of water in its various states as a gas, liquid, and solid; and they should be able to recognize the significance of water within multiple ecosystems. These various layers of interconnectedness are profoundly important to a good education.

But we may also expect students in a Mennonite school to understand and interpret these facts within a *moral* framework. They must wrestle, for example, with the question of whether it is ever legitimate for a Christian to participate in an immoral act (killing another human being in the Civil War) in order to pursue a seemingly moral goal (bringing an end to slavery). Or in the case of the chemistry class, they must recognize in a classroom setting that water is a gift given to us by God, that we have a responsibility to be stewards of this precious resource, and that powerful interests are at stake in public discussions as to how water is allocated and distributed, often to the disadvantage of the poor.

Our efforts to see facts within a larger context will also likely have a *spiritual* component. How, we might ask in a discussion of the Civil War, is God visible in the events of human history? Does God direct the outcome of human activities? Is history moving in the direction of the kingdom of God? Or the science class might take a moment to ponder how the molecules of water so crucial to the flourishing of physical life also signal the presence of God in the ritual of baptism. Even if water happens to be abundant in one's neighborhood, it is still appropriate to treat it with a certain kind of reverence, giving thanks to God each time we are refreshed by a glass of water or watch the rain fall on a thirsty garden.

Cultivating the gift of vision in an Anabaptist-Mennonite context will also shape the way we see ourselves in relationship to other people in the world. The theologian Miroslav Volf has written insightfully about the Christian virtue of "double vision": an ability to see the world both "from here," out of the clarity of our own identity and place and context, and also "from there," from the perspective of the other. Double vision requires a capacity to move across cultural, economic, political, or racial boundaries and to enter imaginatively into the world of someone quite different from ourselves, asking how the insights gleaned from that alternative perspective might help us to see our own world in a clearer way. The modest goal in all of this, writes Volf, is to acquire "a common language, a common human understanding, that will, we hope, in some way approximate the way the all-knowing God, who views things from everywhere, sees both us and them."[17] The goal of this sort of vision is to cultivate the habit of seeing the world through the eyes of Christ in a way that honors differences but refuses to define others by standard categories of national identity, economic power, or social status. This is the gift of seeing the world whole, a world in which "all things" are united in Christ (Col 1:17).

Another expression of vision as a learning outcome in a Mennonite school may be described as the cultivation of an "eschatological perspective." This is a readiness to look upon our own actions or events around us within a context that is anchored in the deep history of God's actions in the past and an awareness of a future that extends beyond the horizon of our understanding. God is at work in history, redeeming all of creation to its intended purposes. Profound changes in the world have come about by the steady, tireless actions of humble individuals who had the audacity to envision a new world.

One Sunday while traveling in Germany, I was invited to preach in a Baptist church in Berlin. I had recently published a book on the gospel of peace, which had been translated into German, and the little congregation wanted to discuss the themes in greater detail. Soon after I began to preach, however, I noticed that an elderly man sitting close to the front had begun to weep. I found this a bit disconcerting but continued my sermon on the centrality of peacemaking to the gospel. At the end of the service, the old man came up to me with a story to tell. As it turned out, the Baptist church was located in a part of Berlin that had belonged to the former East Germany. In 1961 a huge and imposing wall was built, separating East Germany from the rest of the world. Mines lined the area behind the first barbed-wire barriers, and German shepherd dogs and soldiers with machine guns guarded the entire length of the wall.

Every Sunday evening throughout the 1960s and 1970s, the man and a small group of other members gathered in front of the wall that ran close by the church. There they lit candles and held vigils, praying that someday the wall would be removed. People laughed at them, soldiers jeered them, and the man and church group were often discouraged. But they kept gathering. In the 1980s, more and more people began to join them in their candlelight vigils. As political tensions grew, the East German government sent more troops to disperse the crowds. "But with hands shaking in fear," he said, "we continued to hold our candles high."

Then, to the surprise of nearly all the world, on the evening of November 9, 1989, thousands of East Berliners thronged to the border crossings. At 10:30 p.m. the crowd pressed across the border at Bornholmer Strasse, marking the end of the Berlin Wall. "We knew that we could not do this on our own," the old man said, crying once again, "but we waited and prayed. And the wall came down! The wall came down!"

Eschatological vision suggests a willingness to live with both radical hope and radical patience. Radical hope calls us to participate daily in acts that heal the world, no matter how small or seemingly insignificant, in the confidence that we are participating in the larger trajectory of God's purposes being worked out in history. Radical patience suggests that we will not judge each other's faithfulness or God's presence on the basis of short-term outcomes, and that we will be modest and humble about our understanding of God's plans or our capacity to control the outcome of history.

How teachers in Mennonite schools go about cultivating this gift of vision in themselves and in their students will vary enormously, depending on specific gifts, the developmental stage of students, and the context of each classroom. But students in Mennonite schools at all levels should be developing an aptitude for seeing the world more clearly. Teachers should be able to describe how their teaching and assignments are nurturing this gift of vision. And Mennonite schools should be quick to celebrate their alumni who have made a difference in their communities because they see the world in a distinctive way.

2. Touch: Mennonite Education Is Practical, Engaged, and Embodied

In the last chapter of the Gospel of Luke (24:13-27), we read an account of two people walking along a dusty road toward their hometown of Emmaus. Both are followers of Jesus, witnesses to his profound teachings, his miracles of healing, and the hope that he generated in the Jewish people that the Messiah has indeed come. But then they saw the terrible events unfold in Jerusalem. Jesus was arrested, tried, and executed like a common criminal, left to die a slow, humiliating death on the cross. Now with shattered hopes, they dejectedly walk back to their home village.

Along the way a stranger joins them, a teacher obviously well-read in the Jewish Scriptures. When they tell him their story of disappointment—their mistaken hope that the Messiah has come—the stranger rebukes them and lectures them on the Hebrew prophets. "It's all stated very clearly," the stranger insists. "The Messiah must first suffer and die before he can enter into his glory." The two do not understand the explanation. Nonetheless, they invite the stranger-turned-teacher into their home for a meager supper. Then the stranger takes a loaf of bread, blesses it, and passes it to them to eat. And when they receive the bread in their hands, the text says, suddenly "their eyes were opened." Only at the moment of touching the bread do they recognize the risen Jesus in their midst. And just that quickly Jesus vanishes.

This odd story parallels another postresurrection appearance by Jesus, this time recounted in the Gospel of John (20:24-29), in which a disciple named Thomas plays a central role. Like the two on the road to Emmaus, Thomas has heard a theory about Jesus' resurrection. Based on the reports of others, he has an awareness of what is happening. But he still does not really understand the meaning of the event. Thomas needs to confirm the abstract claims about the resurrection with the physical evidence of human touch. When he does so—just like the couple from Emmaus—he suddenly recognizes Jesus, saying, "My Lord and my God!"

Both stories point to an elemental truth about education grounded in an Anabaptist-Mennonite understanding of the incarnation. God is revealed to humans in the
tangible, physical material of creation. Abstract ideas and
words matter—we need to have theory. But there are times
when actually holding the bread or touching the wounds
offers a path to understanding that abstract arguments
cannot communicate. The Christian tradition has labeled
Thomas as "the doubter"; a more sensitive teacher might
have described him as a "tactile learner."

If, as the incarnation affirms, the material world—the
world that we see, taste, smell, and touch—is latent with
the possibility of revealing the presence of Christ, then
education in Mennonite schools should place a high value
on practical, physical engagement with the world, what is
often called "experiential learning."[18]

One expression of this is a willingness to blur the boundaries of the classroom in order to extend the educational context
into the world of nature. In his bestselling book *Last Child
in the Woods*, Richard Louv studies contemporary children
and tracks the decline of their physical contact with nature.
Direct contact with nature, he argues, is essential for healthy
human development.[19] Mennonite schools should consciously
address this growing problem of nature deficiency. Just as
upper-level science courses assume the need for a lab component, elementary school classrooms should be settings where
children become attentive to the changing seasons, where they
directly experience plants and animals, incubated eggs, and
the transformation of cocoons into butterflies; where they
pursue the pleasures of bird-watching, collect leaves, sample
soil, test water, and see the natural world as a crucial part of
their education. Field trips to farms, parks, or environmental
centers are not diversions from *real* learning; they extend the
classroom with opportunities to encounter the presence of
God in the richness of the natural world.

In a similar way, Mennonite schools should provide students with many other opportunities for education outside the classroom, connecting ideas with practical experiences. On the one hand, this is simply good pedagogical practice. Many schools have vocational training of some sort, and virtually all colleges have an internship requirement. But at a deeper level, cultivating the sense of touch points to the Anabaptist conviction that true faith will always find expression in how we live, in the nitty-gritty, practical realities of daily life. In the famous words of the sixteenth-century Anabaptist theologian Hans Denck, "No one can truly know Christ without following him in daily life." This suggests that Mennonite schools should provide students with plenty of opportunities for practical expressions of faith: workdays, mission trips, job shadowing, collaborative research, mentor/mentee programs, and on-site classes.

In the words of Teresa of Avila (1515–82), "Christ has no body but yours; no hands, no feet on earth but yours. Yours are the eyes with which he looks compassion on this world." The creative touches of the mechanic, engineer, architect, carpenter, artist, and seamstress, like that of the social worker, businessperson, doctor, pharmacist, farmer, and nurse are opportunities to participate with God in healing the world.

The point in all this is not to reject more abstract disciplines—philosophy, for example, or higher forms of mathematics. Nor do I want to imply that education must always be practical in a narrow, vocational sense. The experience of touch is never an end in itself. Incarnational touch that leads to transformation is always shaped by an earlier context of knowledge, as it was for the disciple Thomas and for the two disciples on the road to Emmaus.

But because God is revealed to humans in a physical form, we should take seriously the material world and the practical experiences of engaging the material world. Mennonite schools should be educating students in the art of touch.

3. Taste: The Discipline of Discernment

Once, when our first daughter was not quite a year old, we were playing outside after a summer rain when I saw to my horror that she had just put a long earthworm into her mouth. Like all infants at a certain developmental stage, the world for her was filled with fascinating and interesting things, and her primary means of engaging the world was by taste. Everything that looked interesting needed to be tasted. And with good reason: From a very early age our tongues are richly supplied with taste buds.

Tasting things is one of the first means we have of exploring the world around us. Infants confirm their senses of sight and touch by relying on their taste buds to give them more information about what they hold. Even more significantly, our sense of taste is closely associated with the pleasure of eating. We eat food not only for physical survival or merely to satisfy our hunger, but also for the anticipation of the enjoyable sensory experience of taste and texture. To compress all the nutrients supplied in our meals into a pill that we swallow three times a day would be a sad technological development indeed.

But here is also where a certain kind of education begins. When I saw Sarah with an earthworm wriggling in her mouth, my immediate reaction was quick and decisive: "No! Yeeech! No! We don't eat worms!" Part of my task as a parent was to help Sarah understand the difference between the nutritious pleasures of a good meal and those things that might initially feel interesting in her mouth but ultimately would not be to her benefit.

Although the context frequently shifted throughout our years of parenting, my wife and I often repeated similar sorts of admonition to our children. Yes, the world is filled with an endless variety of wonderful and fascinating things; yes, many of them are rich in sustenance and might even taste good at first. But many of the things that children are tempted to ingest are also unhealthy; and some are outright poisonous.

Conversation about *taste* in educational settings, of course, goes far beyond the nutritional value of earthworms or whatever it is that children might be tempted to put into their mouths. When we talk about taste, we are really trying to describe something like mature judgment and discernment: the wisdom necessary to sort out what is appropriate to do, experience, and incorporate into our lives and what should be set aside.

The conversation about taste is complicated by the fact that there are so many confusions swirling around the challenge of wise discernment. Some people, for example, regard taste as purely a matter of personal preference: you like country music, I like gospel; you have a taste for spicy foods, I prefer potatoes and gravy; if someone wants to eat earthworms, figuratively speaking, let her eat earthworms—"It's all a matter of personal taste." To suggest that there are any standards of taste beyond personal preference seems to evoke images of narrow-minded and prudish morality police who "strain out a gnat" (Matt 23:24), or aesthetic snobs who sneer at anyone who fails to appreciate their refined taste for classical music or modern art. Taste, for some people, is merely the consensus opinion of one particular group that is trying to impose its standards on everyone else.

As a consequence, some people, perhaps especially young people, are inclined to taste everything there is to consume: if it is accessible, it should be tried, they think. Movies that allow us to experience vicariously the thrill of a chase scene, the profound terror of imminent death, the intimacies of forbidden love, or the sheer lust of sexual desire all activate the taste buds of pleasure. The problem is that once activated, our taste buds desire more stimulation, and we find ourselves pulled into the ever-escalating thrill of sensory excitement. Without really noticing, our emotional and moral sensitivity begins to dull. What once terrified us in a scene where violence was only threatened or implied now seems passé; so the movie industry needs to up the ante with images of chainsaws dismembering bodies. The thrill of a romantic prelude to a kiss now seems embarrassingly tame; so our voyeuristic desires are increasingly ratcheted in the direction of outright pornography. Shocking images, outrageous behavior, or thrilling experiences trigger deep emotions because we are aware that they are transgressing a moral boundary. But once all boundaries have been repeatedly transgressed, we are left with a loss of taste—an inner emptiness, a moral vacuum, and an inability to discern subtle differences or nuances or fine distinctions about what we are seeing or hearing.

A different and seemingly more benign impulse in modern culture is to avoid the hard work of discernment by embracing a culture of kitsch. If the shock culture of the entertainment industry seeks to break down all boundaries of taste, a culture of kitsch remains resolutely safe within those same clearly-established boundaries. Kitsch—whether in music, art, literature, or faith—is by definition imitative and predictable. It resides in the nostalgic safety of memories. It avoids all mystery by self-consciously repeating established formulas that have yielded specific emotional reactions in the past. If shock culture denies that there is a God, kitsch makes an idol out of human creations. It trades off the living mystery of the incarnation for the sentimental comfort and security of a golden calf made by human hands.

From an educational perspective, taste—the art of discriminating between bad, good, better, and best—is something that must be learned. It must be cultivated and practiced. This means that students in Mennonite schools should have opportunities to try lots of different things and to encounter many people and experiences. Overly picky eaters, content to live on macaroni and cheese, miss out on the rich, wonderful variety of exotic spices and cross-cultural cuisine. Part of the task of church-related education is to help students broaden their palates, but in such a way that they do not swallow everything that comes their way. Not everything that tastes good initially is healthy. So developing good taste means that we learn what is nourishing and what to spit out.

The goal in all this is to become critics in the best sense of the word—not the critical posture of a cynic, and not the critical attitude of an elite snob. What we are looking for instead is something closer to what Paul admonishes the church in Philippi: "Whatever is true, whatever is noble, whatever is right, whatever is pure, whatever is lovely, whatever is admirable—if anything is excellent or praiseworthy—think about such things. Whatever you have learned or received or heard from me, or seen in me—put it into practice. And the God of peace will be with you" (Phil 4:8-9).

Taste can rarely be reduced to a set of rules or rigid definitions. But there are some resources. One beginning point for an education in taste is simply a careful consideration of the consequences of our choices. What we ingest—literally or figuratively—can significantly affect our well-being. Smoking three packs of cigarettes every day for twenty years, for example, is likely to lead to lung cancer. So raising questions about the merits of smoking is not just a matter of personal taste, but also a reminder that this choice has real consequences for your own health, for the well-being of those around you, and for the larger society, which will be saddled with paying medical expenses that could have been avoided.

Education also provides us with historical perspectives on our judgments, perspectives that contribute to discernment. Contemporaries of Socrates did not think highly of his philosophical ideas and tried to silence him by forcing him to drink poison. Nonetheless, more than two millennia later, people are still reading his dialogues, discovering anew Socrates's insightful observations about questions related to human nature, human community, and other big themes like goodness, truth, and beauty. Not everyone agrees with Socrates; but whereas thousands of other writers have long been forgotten, we continue to be attracted to his thought. When it comes to thinking carefully about profound questions of justice, Socrates provides one standard that informs and educates our taste. His ideas matter, in part at least, because a lot of people for a long time have regarded them as having merit.

We also develop discriminating taste by studying exemplary people. While public education focuses on national heroes as the models, Mennonite schools cultivate good taste by focusing on the heroes of Christian virtue: saints and martyrs who best embody the characteristics that we want to imitate. Ultimately the example that matters most is the one set by Jesus. "Have the same attitude as Christ," Paul wrote to the Philippians (2:5).

Mennonite schools should be places where students cultivate good taste by practicing the skills of discernment. This happens in many ways, but it always includes a deep understanding of Scripture as informed by the stories of tradition and the teachings of the church; a conscious attentiveness to the wisdom of teachers and mentors; and practice in the spiritual disciplines of listening for the voice of the Holy Spirit, in the context of the Christian community.

4. Hearing: Learning to Listen to Others and to God

In the Old Testament we read the intriguing story of the education of a young man named Samuel. Even before Samuel is born, his mother Hannah has dedicated him to God. When he is still a child, she sends him to the temple in Shiloh, to serve as a student-in-training with Eli the priest (1 Sam 2–3). Eli is Samuel's mentor, charged with the task of training him in the traditions of the covenant, in hearing the word of the Lord, and in the various responsibilities of a priest. One night, while still barely more than a boy, Samuel is awakened by a voice calling his name. Three times he goes to Eli, thinking his teacher is calling him. Finally Eli redirects Samuel's attention: "It's not me calling you; . . . perhaps it's the Lord." So the next time Samuel hears a voice calling his name, he turns his attention to God: "Speak, LORD, for your servant is listening." And the Lord speaks to Samuel: "See, I am about to do something in Israel that will make both ears of everyone who hears it tingle" (3:9-11 NRSV).

Samuel's calling as a prophet cannot be reduced to this single incident. After all, his mother has dedicated him to God's service from the beginning of his life. Moreover, Samuel has the good fortune of receiving a spiritual education from an expert in the field; Eli plays a crucial role in helping Samuel know how to be attentive to God's leading.

But in the end, Samuel does not understand his true calling until he actively listens to the voice of God.

The human sense of hearing, like sight and taste, is one of the most basic ways we engage the world. Sounds fill the world. From the moment of birth babies hear traffic noise, dogs barking, fans humming, trees rustling, radio news reports, TV sitcoms, and the ringtones of countless cell phones.

As infants we are especially attuned to the intimate voices of our parents, siblings, extended family, and friends. As we become more attentive in our listening, we begin to separate those sounds by hearing the distinct intonation of individual words. Slowly we learn how to decode the meaning associated with those words. And then over time our ears become more adept at hearing even the deeper, hidden meanings of speech, conveyed by the subtleties of intonation, nuance, and context.

Listening precedes speaking. For many of us, learning to speak actually diminishes the acuity of our sense of hearing.

As with "looking" and "seeing," there is a difference between simply "hearing" and truly "listening." We hear noises all the time. Listening, by contrast, is the posture of mindful attentiveness by which we seek to understand the sounds that we hear. When teachers say, "Listen up!" or "Please be quiet and listen to me," or reproach students with the words "Why weren't you listening?" they can be sure their students have been hearing their voices all along; but true listening assumes a relationship of active and intentional communication.

Listening is a skill that can be learned. When I was in high school, I was virtually tone-deaf. This was a source of great bewilderment to my family, especially my mother, who was a very gifted musician with a lovely singing voice. My siblings could sing, but I simply had no confidence in being able to follow a part or stay in tune. Then at some point during a music class in high school, we were required to sing excerpts from Handel's *Messiah*. The teacher placed me, rather arbitrarily I think, with the tenors. Over and over again we listened to recordings of *Messiah*, and then to a pianist playing just the tenor part. Gradually I began to hear the distinctive tenor line within the larger harmony of the chorus. With even more time and practice, I began to hear my own voice singing along, more or less in tune.

For me it was a breakthrough experience. Although I never have become a gifted singer, I now have an inner ear that enables me to hear the part that I am supposed to sing. Over time, with lots more practice, singing has become easier and easier.

Mennonite schools will foster in their students the gift of listening. Listening begins with a sense of curiosity and respect—an awareness that what others are saying might be of interest and that I might learn something from them that I did not know before. Anyone who has given a speech knows how disheartening it is to see members of the audience stretched out with their eyes closed, or whispering to others, or gazing absent-mindedly out the window. Active listening—a posture of attentiveness with appropriate eye contact and facial expressions—honors the speaker. Active listening is not simply patient endurance until someone has stopped speaking, so that you can begin to speak. It implies a posture of engaged empathy that genuinely seeks to enter into the experience of someone else and to learn more by asking probing questions. Active listeners are always attentive to the voices not being heard in a conversation and gently seek them out. Active listeners are less concerned with defending a position than they are with understanding the perspective of the other person. Indeed, sometimes the experience of silence, having the gift of knowing when not to talk, can also be an act of listening.

For educators in Mennonite schools, cultivating the gift of listening will likely include some conscious practice. For young children, learning how to take turns when speaking may start out as a rule, but eventually that rule grows into a deeper appreciation and respect for each classmate, along with a desire to know what others have to say. One discipline for attentive listening is simply to practice experiencing extended silences, where students listen carefully to background sounds that they have not noticed before—to the sound of their own heartbeats, or to the sound of silence itself.

It may be useful to structure discussions so that each person must summarize what the preceding speaker said before adding one's own opinion. Other forms of listening include the skill of careful reading, so that the reader is committed to understanding what the author is saying even if the reader disagrees from the outset with the position being defended. A critical awareness of the partisan nature of public discourse is yet another form of listening, as is the skill of eliciting voices from students who otherwise tend to remain silent.

At an even deeper level, teachers in Mennonite schools nurturing the gift of listening in their students will play the role of Eli. They will actively encourage students to be attentive to the voice of God, who is inviting them, like he did Samuel, to devote their lives to God's service. This can happen in many ways: structured prayer, silent reflection, spiritual disciplines, or direct counseling. In this process of discernment, the challenge is not to speak for God, but, like Eli, to prepare students to hear at the moment when God is calling.

5. Voice: Discovering Our Vocation

One of the many pleasures of teaching over a long period of time is the opportunity to become reacquainted with students at later stages in their lives. When I first met Mandy, she had the frightened look of a person who clearly felt as if she did not belong on a college campus. In class, she sat in the back of the room, quickly pulled her books together when the period was over, and then slipped out of sight. Her written work was excellent; if I called on her directly, she would respond, albeit hesitantly and quietly. It was clear that she was doing her homework and was mentally engaged in the class. But one day when she was giving a small oral presentation to the rest of the class, her hands began shaking uncontrollably. Only with great effort did she make her presentation, and then in a voice barely above a whisper. When I talked with her on the sidewalk or in my office, she often had interesting things to say, but she almost always spoke quietly, eyes directed downward.

Several years ago, I ran into Mandy again. I was attending a conference and discovered, to my great surprise, that Mandy was listed as one of the presenters. I assumed that it was a case of another person by the same name. But when I got to the session, I immediately recognized her. Over the years she had become the executive director of a not-for-profit organization that linked artisans in Central America with wholesalers in the United States. She gave a powerful presentation on her organization and responded with clarity and humor during the question-and-answer time. I was stunned and deeply moved. Could this really be the same person I recalled some fifteen years earlier as an excruciatingly shy first-year student?

In our conversation afterward, the mystery was slowly resolved. A key moment in her transformation had happened during a college study-service term in Honduras. She had been assigned to live with a host family that was gregarious, loving, warm, and funny. They did not know her as a shy person and simply swept her along to family events, chalking up any hesitance she might have expressed to her cross-cultural confusion. It turned out that she loved Spanish and became practically fluent by the end of the three-month term. After returning home, she remained in contact with her host family, visiting them the following summer and then again for a longer period of time after graduation.

During her visits Mandy renewed contacts with local artisans where she had done her service assignment. Slowly, collaborating with an organization already established in the area, she built up a program that connected artisans with stores in the United States. Along the way, churches and other groups invited her to speak about her experience and she discovered—almost to her own surprise—that she had a story to tell. "I found a passion," Mandy said. With it, she found her voice.

Like taste, sight, or hearing, our voices are a crucial means by which we engage the world. Every baby announces its presence with a cry and continues to communicate its basic needs with grunts, coos, and screams. But soon enough, a baby learns to laugh; then the infant slowly begins to imitate the sounds heard, tracking the delight of parents who respond to its voice.

Eventually every child discovers that voices have power. Words connect us to a broader community. They enable us to communicate basic needs and desires. Words have the power to wound or to heal; they can curse as well as bless; they can offend or inspire. Our voices become an extension of ourselves through the power of persuasive speech, the burst of laughter, murmured gossip, a gentle admonition, a fervent prayer, a word of encouragement.

Mennonite schools will help students find their voice. Each of our students has a name that bears within it a unique treasure. Each has been entrusted with a unique voice—a distinctive inflection, dialect, or song—that is shared by no one else. At the same time, Mennonite schools will cultivate an awareness in students that the gifts given to each of us are meant to be shared. Our voices are meant to be heard. Sometimes this happens in the close harmonies of a chorale or in the quiet reason of reconciler. Sometimes it is the voice of the poet who gives expression to the invisible or the utopian who dreams of new worlds. It could be the voice of the lawyer and legislator, who learn the language of the legal system, or that of the preacher, teacher, and missionary. Sometimes the voice will be heard in the sharp—maybe even strident—language of the prophet who denounces racism and injustice, exposes hypocrisy, and challenges the status quo. Or it may be the voice of the translator, who stands with feet in two cultures, bridging worlds that otherwise are incomprehensible to each other.

Mennonite schools should consciously set themselves the goal of helping students discover their vocations or calling. The word *vocation* comes from the Latin, meaning "to be called out"—to be named by God for a particular mission. To find our calling is to discover our voice.

6. Smell: Being Attentive to the Presence of the Unseen

Following my first year of college, I dropped out of school and took a job, working on a small farm in a tiny village of Austria. For the first time in my life, I was immersed in a religious culture completely different from my own. Every Sunday I went with my family to mass in the local Catholic church. In many ways the service seemed strange to me, but I was deeply impressed by the way in which the mass appealed to every sense, including the sense of smell. As the priest prepared to consecrate the wafer just before communion, he or one of the altar boys would carefully swing a censer, filled with burning incense. The smell filled the little church, sometimes burning my eyes.

Initially the ritual seemed strange. But over time the smell of incense became for me a powerful symbol for the presence of the Holy Spirit—a presence not visible to the eye, yet a reality.

Smell is perhaps the most elusive of the senses. Unlike many animals with a highly sensitive capacity for smell, humans do not rely on it very much. Compared with sight, hearing, or touch, it is likely to be the sense least well developed. Yet smell can trigger a sudden alertness in us. "Do you smell something?" we might ask on entering the kitchen after being gone for a while, wondering if the gas stove may have developed a leak in our absence. So we pause, sniff a bit more, and then move on. The faintest whiff of perfume can heighten our senses, drawing us closer to another person without our understanding why.

Smell is profoundly evocative; it is the sense most clearly linked to memory. Anyone who suddenly encounters the sweet smell of a newly mown hayfield, a whiff of freshly baked cookies, the wafting scent of spring flowers, the pungent odor of a skunk, or the delicate aromas of certain spices—that person is likely to experience long-forgotten memories surging to the surface.

Like unbidden memories, smell is not something fully rational. One might say that it is "precognitive." It triggers our intuition, a sense of something that cannot always be rationally defended or put into precise language. If we are suspicious of something, without really knowing why, we might say, "Something doesn't smell quite right about this."

That the sense of smell would have any bearing whatsoever on a philosophy of education—even one framed in the language of the incarnation—may seem to be a stretch of the imagination. Nonetheless, I suggest that Mennonite schools, shaped by the reality of the incarnation, will cultivate students who are attuned to the elusive qualities associated with smell.

There is a reality that goes beyond what we can see, hear, taste, and touch. There is a reality that we cannot fully apprehend, but it is no less real. Being attentive to this reality calls us to trust our intuitions, to heed our inner nudges, to discern the movement of the Holy Spirit even if it is sensed only dimly. Poets, artists, and musicians are often tuned to this mysterious moving of the Holy Spirit. Their work invites us to explore the wonder, mystery, and awe that often elude our ability to contain, define, or capture.

Living a life fully attuned to the Spirit, like the swinging censer of the Catholic priest, will spread a fragrance that bears witness to the Spirit within. The apostle Paul understands this elusive, but powerful, witness as he writes to the church at Corinth: "But thanks be to God, who . . . through us spreads everywhere the fragrance of the knowledge of Christ. For we are to God the aroma of Christ among those who are being saved. . . . And who is equal to such a task?" (2 Cor 2:14-16).

Some educational theorists have suggested that teachers should begin planning for any course by writing the final exam and only then stepping back to design the curriculum. Teachers in Mennonite schools might ask themselves: How would my teaching change if I start with these outcomes—habits of vision, taste, hearing, touch, voice, and smell attuned to the presence of God—and create a curriculum that is focused on *these* sensory goals? What would it look like if the state standards of content and skills for my grade level or discipline were understood not as the primary end goal, but as merely the raw material for helping students pursue these more qualitative outcomes?

In a similar vein, school principals might ask themselves: How might we give public recognition to students who are making life-shaping choices in the direction of God's healing work in creation? We are accustomed to honoring students with a dean's list; what might it look like to honor students for qualities like stewardship, empathy, graciousness, joy, peacemaking, or service?

Assessment: How Do We Know If We Are Making a Difference?

Students of all ages who participate in Mennonite education should be cultivating their senses of sight, taste, hearing, touch, speaking, and smell in a special way. Our physical senses can also serve as windows to the spirit. They are the bridges by which we can become attentive to God's incarnated presence in the world. If you ask what the "value-added" contribution of Mennonite education might be—or how the education a student receives at a Mennonite school is any different from what they could expect at a public institution—one way it should be evident is in these qualities.

If these are the right outcomes to expect from an Anabaptist-Mennonite education, how will we know if they are actually being learned? What is the evidence for this?

Here Mennonite schools will find themselves with a foot in two different worlds. On the one hand, we cannot ignore arguments demanding greater accountability and more careful assessment. After all, as most educators know, there is a crucial difference between teaching and learning. Instructors can insist that they have taught the lesson, but if one does not have an effective method for determining whether or not students actually *learned* the lesson, then the claims of the teacher ring hollow. Teachers might be correct in their insistence that instruction is happening, but that does not necessarily mean that students are being educated. Pressures in our culture to demonstrate educational success with quantifiable measures are not entirely misplaced. Mennonite schools should never use the distinctive nature of their mission as an excuse for mediocrity in assessing basic competencies or the content of a subject area.

Yet the impulse to reduce educational outcomes to quantifiable measures that conform to standard test-taking strategies often fails to capture precisely the qualities that we care most about in a church-related education. This tension between conformity to external standards and the more elusive ideals of virtuous life runs deep in the Christian story. At one point in Jesus' ministry, several Pharisees, experts in the Jewish educational system, come to Jesus looking for a clear answer from him regarding his curriculum. One of them, highly trained in the law, "tested him with this question: 'Teacher, which is the greatest commandment in the Law?'" Jesus' response is clear: "'Love the Lord your God with all your heart and with all your soul and with all your mind.' This is the first and greatest commandment. And the second is like it: 'Love your neighbor as yourself.'" That is the summary of what matters most for Jesus. In fact, he concludes by saying, "All the Law and the Prophets hang on these two commandments" (Matt 22:35-40).

On another occasion, Jesus addresses the question of essentials by calling his listeners' attention to the final day of judgment. Those who will be saved, Jesus declares, are not those who know the right answers (the ones who say "Lord, Lord") but those who "[do] the will of my Father." The true test at the final judgment day will be the quality of the fruit that one bears. "A good tree cannot bear bad fruit, and a bad tree cannot bear good fruit. . . . Thus, by their fruit you will recognize them" (Matt 7:18-22).

Educators are gardeners, assisting in the cultivation of living vines that will ultimately bear fruit. Although the miracle of life is not in our hands, we play a vital role in that process. We may do our task poorly, possibly even cause great harm. But our goal is to nurture the life, health, and wholeness of the plants entrusted to us. This means keeping the weeds at bay and watching out for pests. It also means paying special attention to each plant and the combination of soil and fertilizer that best promotes its growth.

In the end, however, it is not the gardener who brings forth the fruit. A plant flourishes and bears fruit only if it remains connected to the vine that gives and sustains life. In the words of Psalm 34:8, "Taste and see that the Lord is good."

Keeping the Conversation Alive:
Addressing Tough Questions

One spring afternoon I received a phone call from a Mennonite pastor in an area I had recently visited. For many years Joe's congregation had been a stalwart supporter of Mennonite education, especially the local Mennonite K–12 school. Promotional brochures were always visible in the lobby of their church. School choirs frequently visited the congregation. Church members volunteered at the school's annual fundraisers and the congregation generously supported the school through their budget and a tuition partnership plan.

But according to the pastor, the enthusiastic support that had once seemed so self-evident was now slowly eroding. Parents of youth who attended local public schools had begun to express concern that their children felt pushed to the margins. This was not intentional, but informal talk and social activity outside the youth group meetings revolved around activities at the Mennonite school. For several years the congregation had struggled to meet its budget. Now what had once been only an undercurrent of grumbling at church business meetings was turning into open doubts about the percentage of the church budget that was being directed to Mennonite education. As tuition costs continued to climb, some members began to compare those figures unfavorably with the amount that the congregation was committing to missions.

And, Joe continued, other concerns had surfaced. In the past year the parents of a child with disabilities learned to their disappointment that the school did not have adequate staffing to provide support at a level comparable to that of the public schools. At about the same time, a student attending the Mennonite school was disciplined for violating a school policy. Her parents regarded the punishment as unfair and registered their concerns to their Sunday school class. In the same Sunday school class, several members of the congregation who were public school teachers used the occasion to express resentment about the judgmentalism implicit in the choice made against public education. They felt as though their service as a Christian witness in the public school was not valued. The church school option, they suggested, was a retreat from the "real world."

Support for the school that had once seemed so self-evident was clearly waning. When the local public high school basketball team went to the state tournament, the whole community was caught up in the excitement. Children in the congregation talked excitedly about the team and wore shirts bearing the school's insignia. Among young families in the church, the sentiment seemed to be turning against sending their children to the Mennonite school.

Now Joe was feeling pressure to hold together a divided congregation. The arguments that had once seemed so obvious in favor of Mennonite education were no longer as clear. "I feel like I'm in a complete bind," he said. "On the one hand, I really believe in Christian education. I think it's the right thing for our children and for the future of the church. I want to support Mennonite education. On the other hand, I can understand the concerns of those who are sending their children to the public school. For me to give visible support to the Mennonite school would only deepen the conflict."

It is always risky to generalize from a single story. Every

congregation has a different experience in the history of their attitude toward church-related education. Yet even though the issues raised do not lend themselves to simple, clear, or even right answers, the concerns Joe listed were honest and the tensions expressed in his congregation were genuine.

In this chapter I offer a beginning response to some of the tough questions about Mennonite education that often emerged in conversations among parents, pastors, teachers, board members, and administrators. As in other chapters, my intention in offering these responses is not to be defensive or definitive. To be sure, I wish to make the case in favor of Mennonite education. But my goal is to move the conversation forward in a clear and healthy way, not to put an end to the discussion with airtight arguments.

Addressing Tough Questions: For Parents

1. What Difference Does It Make If I Send My Children to a Mennonite School?

Parents looking for a guarantee that sending their child to a Mennonite school will result in a great job, unwavering Christian faith, and a lifetime of service to the church are likely to be disappointed. Although several studies suggest that attending Mennonite schools is clearly correlated with an increased likelihood of going on to serve the church in some aspect of ministry—such as voluntary service, mission work, the pastorate, or denominational leadership—*correlation* is not the same thing as *causation*. That is to say, no study has demonstrated with absolute certainty that attendance at a Mennonite school is the single, crucial variable linked in a statistically significant way to a predictable vocational or religious outcome. It is possible, for example, that the same nurturing families and supportive congregations who advocate on behalf Mennonite education for their children also play a central role in shaping a life trajectory that leads to service in the church.

Just as a seed requires a wondrously complex combination of variables if it is to germinate and flourish, so too the nurture of Christian faith in young people depends on many factors. Every gardener knows that some variables are beyond their control. But creating the optimal conditions for growth goes a long way toward improving the chances for an ideal outcome.

Consider this: Anyone who has been a parent realizes that the task of raising a child is overwhelming if everything rests on the shoulders of the parents alone. During the first five years of a child's life, the tasks of parenting are often shared with extended family, close friends, or church members. But in our culture the primary context for the education of our children after the age of five or so takes a dramatic turn. It is not as if parents are no longer involved, but once a child enters kindergarten, the parental role shifts considerably. For the next twelve or sixteen years—during some of the most formative years of a person's life—parents entrust the education of their child into the hands of the state. For nine to ten months of the year, most of a child's waking hours are no longer spent at home, but at school.

Moreover, public schools in the United States are legally bound to frame that education in an explicitly secular mode—to ensure that the context and content of public education is not visibly influenced by any sort of religious commitments. I would never suggest that public school settings are evil or that children educated in public schools are being brainwashed into a worldview devoid of faith. But if I, as a parent, am committed to a particular set of religious and ethical convictions—convictions that have profoundly shaped my view of the world and my frame of reference for moral decision making—then I also want my children to spend this formative period of their lives in the company of teachers who share these same basic values. And I want my children to be immersed in a curriculum that reflects these convictions. I want my child to form lasting relationships with peers whose families are also committed to a similar education.

Attendance at a Mennonite school does not mean that your child will automatically become a Christian, act ethically in every circumstance, remain forever in the church. But sustained nurture in a Christian community of like-minded adults and peers clearly helps to tip the trajectory of development. It is one important variable in the larger complex, dynamic environment within which young people orient their lives and make foundational decisions about their future.

The context and content of education matters. It is one of many investments that parents make for their child's future even though no admissions counselor can with absolute certainty guarantee how any individual child will respond to that educational environment.

2. How Much Is a Mennonite Education Worth? What Is the Financial "Tipping Point"?

For families struggling with mortgage payments, health insurance premiums, and the basic necessities of daily life, budgeting thousands of dollars for tuition at a Mennonite school can seem like an overwhelming challenge—especially when the public school alternative is free and public universities are generally cheaper than Mennonite colleges. These are fair concerns, and at some level they can only be addressed on the basis of individual circumstances. But here are a few things to consider.

During recent decades the cost of education in all schools—public and private—has risen faster than the overall inflation rate. Education in every setting has become more expensive. One factor driving up tuition costs in Mennonite schools has been steadily rising expectations on the part of students and parents. We have come to expect well-maintained facilities, small class sizes, the latest technology, a full array of course options, lots of extracurricular options, and salaries for teachers and administrators that are commensurate with the local public schools. Indeed, the real cost of education today is actually much higher than can be met with tuition income alone. Administrators face pressures to generate additional money through direct contributions, annual fundraisers, and endowment income. When these sources of revenue are tight, tuition increases often make up the difference. The risk is that Mennonite schools will eventually become affordable only to the wealthy.

In the face of these challenges what are the options? First, schools almost always have some need-based financial aid available. This comes in various forms. Sometimes the school offers a straightforward scholarship, funded by an endowment or generous patrons. Sometimes the school helps to facilitate low-interest loans for families with financial need. Other times grandparents or extended family members subsidize tuition, or older students supplement their own tuition with income from summer and after-school jobs. Occasionally schools establish a form of labor exchange in which family members can work off a portion of the tuition expenses by tending the grounds or doing custodial or office work.

Traditionally, however, the biggest form of tuition support has come from local congregations. Most schools have established partnership plans with supporting congregations to help spread the cost of education. These plans are often understood to supplement tuition costs for parents, not to absorb the full amount. But the additional support is often the crucial difference in deciding whether or not to enroll. In the words of the familiar proverb, "It takes a village to raise a child." In modern contexts one role of the village is to share the financial costs of church-based education. Partnership plans are an opportunity to practice mutual aid within congregations. Such support invests in the lives of young people and in the future of the church.

Finally, meeting the financial challenges of church-related education often comes down to a question of priorities. How important is this decision to you and your family? Individual circumstances vary greatly; yet in comparison with most of the world, North Americans have a great deal of discretionary income, especially if we calculate how much we currently spend on things like cell phone plans, satellite TV, video rentals, eating out, vacationing or expensive cars. We usually do not think in these terms, but a three-dollar cup of Starbucks coffee every morning adds up to more than a thousand dollars a year.

Our budgets reflect our priorities. We spend our money on what matter most to us. In most instances, families committed to sending their children to Mennonite schools can find a way to do so, even if it may mean some rearranged financial priorities.

3. Why Should I Pay Taxes That Support Public Education and Also Pay Tuition?

In most states Mennonite schools receive little if any public money. Thus, the portion of federal, state, and local taxes that parents pay to support public education does not directly benefit families who send their children to Mennonite schools.

Even though the financial logic of this concern might be clear, it is equally clear that we are part of communities that are bigger than just our congregation or the local Mennonite school. Regardless of whether or not we support church-related education, all Christians should "seek the welfare of the city" (Jer 29:7 NRSV) and promote the well-being of our communities, including local public schools. Strong support for Mennonite schools should never be in tension with a desire for the best education possible in the public school system.

Although some advocates of church-related schooling have lobbied hard for a government voucher system that would enable parents to bring tax dollars to the elementary or high schools of their choice, including Christian private schools, those in the Anabaptist-Mennonite tradition may have legitimate reservations about such initiatives. Beyond the principle of church and state separation (e.g., not having public tax dollars fund a church-based curriculum), it may actually be a good thing for Mennonite schools to remain dependent on contributions from individuals and congregations. Such dependency helps to maintain higher levels of accountability to the church, a stronger base of engaged patron support, and fewer layers of obligation back to the government regarding the school's distinctive policies, curriculum, and commitments.

The picture is somewhat different at the college or university level. For many years, some kinds of state and federal funds have been available to church-related colleges. Thus on an individual basis, college students might qualify for state or federal tuition scholarships, loans, or work-study programs administered by the school. And Mennonite colleges occasionally receive direct grants from the government, generally for initiatives related to technology or facilities, especially in the sciences. So some tax dollars do support church-related schools, although usually indirectly.

In any case, it is certainly possible to both strongly affirm the option of Mennonite education and support public education.

4. Wouldn't It Be a Stronger Missional Witness to Send Our Children to Public Schools?

One argument against Mennonite education—especially in the elementary and high school years—comes from congregational members who regard sending their children to the local public schools as a form of Christian witness. Withdrawing children from the public schools seems to diminish our potential to be "salt and light" in this important public setting.

This argument, which sounds reasonable and noble, is worth examining more closely. Support for church-related education should not be misunderstood as antagonism against the public school. Most supporters of Christian education will continue to pay taxes that support the local school district, and it is likely that many in their congregations will serve the public schools as administrators, teachers, or support staff. But the question of what it means to be *missional* is more complex than this critique usually implies.

In the first place, the argument that our elementary or high school children should be "salt and light" in the public schools—especially in the elementary and high school years—may overlook too quickly the fact that first missional task of all Christian parents is within their own homes: for those in a believers church tradition who do not baptize babies, children are the first mission field. The argument tends to be overly optimistic about the level of Christian formation that is currently happening at home and in the church. It assumes that children are already formed, committed, and mature Christians— that Christian nurture at home and in the congregation has already been sufficient to form the character of individual children in such a way that they are prepared to give a Christian witness in settings where they could be in the minority.

In some instances, this may well be the case. But it is also possible that this scenario is simply wishful thinking on the part of parents. Christian formation in the Anabaptist-Mennonite tradition is not simply a matter of evoking a verbal response from a child who may say, "Yes, I want to follow Jesus." Both a public confession of faith and baptism are crucial moments along the way, but these actions do not instantly turn our children into missionaries. Young Christians need exposure to Scripture. They need practice in integrating Scripture into daily decision making. They need to grow into the habits of viewing the world through the lens of their own commitment to Christ.

The argument may also place a level of Christian accountability on children that parents have not chosen for themselves. One test of this argument is to ask ourselves about the nature of our Christian witness in our own work setting. How easy is it for me to talk freely about my faith or to invite my coworkers to church? If we hesitate to respond, how realistic is it to expect this of children?

The point here is not that children need to be protected at all costs from exposure to a hostile world, nor that we need to pass some standard of Christian maturity before we can testify to our faith. But it may be naive and even disingenuous for parents to insist on sending their children to public schools in the role of missionary witnesses.

5. If Children Don't Go to Public School, How Will They Learn to Defend Their Own Convictions?

A closely related concern suggests that sending children to a Mennonite school will artificially isolate them from the realities of the world. Church schools, the argument goes, are a bubble. They shield our children from the real world.

Even though this concern may initially sound compelling, it is not very convincing. First, few young people today are truly isolated from the world in any meaningful sense, regardless of where they go to school. The powerful realities of technology, mass media, and advertisements virtually guarantee that all young people are deeply shaped in some way by modern culture.

Second, church-related schools are not islands. We certainly do expect the culture of a Mennonite school to be different from that of a public school. Yet today students at all the church schools come from diverse backgrounds, and they experience the same challenges of adolescence and young adult life as their public school peers. Their insecurities can lead to eating disorders or depression; drugs and alcohol tempt them; and the profound pain of divorce, domestic violence, and sexual abuse overwhelm them at times. The point of a church-related school is not to isolate students from these realities, but rather to respond to them from a distinctive frame of reference. It makes a difference, for example, if the students' primary counsel regarding teenage sexuality is framed in the form of medical warnings about STDs and admonitions to practice safe sex, or whether it is anchored in a view of our bodies as made in the image of God, an understanding of relationships grounded on dignity, and a respect for each other that reflects the character of Christ.

All this may sound idealistic. There is no guarantee that students at Mennonite schools will always respond appropriately to the challenges they face. But young people in Mennonite schools do encounter the temptations and confusions of sin and they have ample opportunities to defend their own convictions. The hope is that they will do so in the context of mentors who model alternatives to the social norms, who provide a language for seeing through the illusions of the world, and who embrace them in a community that is willing to hold them accountable for their actions as well as forgive them and restore them back into the community when they make mistakes.

6. If Children Don't Go to Public School, How Will They Be Exposed to Cross-cultural Diversity?

Another variation of this concern is that children attending church-related schools have fewer opportunities to be exposed to the racial, cultural, economic, and religious diversity of the local community. By associating only with the monoculture of white, ethnic Mennonites, the argument goes, they miss out on the richness and complexities of social life in the real world.

This description might be true as a cultural memory; and it may still be the case for a few schools today. But most contemporary Mennonite schools reflect the diversity of the communities of which they are a part. Indeed, they tend to be ahead of many public schools in promoting a deeper awareness of cross-cultural realities and global or international perspectives.

It should also be clear that proximity to cultural diversity is not the same as meaningful cross-cultural interaction. Visit the cafeteria of a public high school, or look at the composition of the advanced placement classes, club memberships, marching band, honor society, or participants in enrichment language trips. These settings are almost always culturally quite segregated. Merely attending a school with culturally diverse students is not the same thing as thoughtful encounters with the reality of ethnic and cultural diversity.

In addition to the growing racial, cultural, and economic diversity evident in many MEA schools, Mennonite schools also offer their students opportunities for service trips, community volunteer projects and for exploring the richness of cross-cultural, international relationships. Many faculty and staff at Mennonite schools have spent a portion of their lives in service, relief work, or missions outside North America. Their pedagogy and classrooms reflect these experiences. Classroom assignments focusing on many cultures and a larger awareness of the world beyond national borders promotes a healthy respect for differences and fosters a worldview that is deeply informed by a commitment to treat all people as children of God. If this is true of Mennonite middle schools and high schools, it is even more the case for Mennonite colleges and universities, which often include cross-cultural service experiences as part of the general education requirement, incorporate international themes throughout their curriculum, and enroll a significant number of international students.

All these efforts do not mean that students always internalize habits of cross-cultural respect and sensitivity. Yet there is no evidence to suggest that students in Mennonite educational settings have significantly less exposure to cultural diversity than their public school counterparts.

Addressing Tough Questions: For Pastors and Congregations

1. What Do We Do About the Tensions within the Congregation among Families Who Have Made Different Decisions?

Congregations that support Mennonite education in one form or another will also have members in their midst whose children attend public schools or universities. Few congregations are unanimous in their support for church-related education. Because the decision to attend a church school is clearly framed within the context of Christian nurture and always involves a real financial commitment, the probability of some sort of conflict within the congregation over these decisions is rather high.

The nature of these tensions can go either way. Sometimes those who attend Mennonite schools feel as if they are in the minority and must defend their choice to peers and fellow members. Other times the public school students and families feel isolated and marginalized—implicitly judged—by those who have opted for church-based schools. Resolving these tensions calls for a great deal of wisdom and sensitivity, especially for pastors and youth leaders who are often more aware of underlying conflicts than are parents or older members who are somewhat removed from social dynamics.

Tensions like these can exist not only between the church/public school options, but also among students who are attending various public school districts. Clearly, congregations need to express support for the activities, accomplishments, and well-being of all young people in the congregation. Youth sponsors should monitor the public attention given to plays, musical events, fundraisers, sports, and academic achievements—making sure that all schools are given appropriate visibility. Youth groups should make a point of attending events at all the schools in support of each student.

Congregations committing resources to church schools do so because they believe them to be a good option. They should not apologize for their decision. But healthy congregations will recognize that individual circumstances differ, and the church should commit itself to respecting and honoring the decisions made by individual families.

2. What Percent of the Church Budget Should Go to Mennonite Schools?

How much of a congregation's budget should be dedicated to Christian education is a question fraught with the potential for conflict. As in marriage, arguments about money are often the most treacherous terrain for relationships within congregations. Budgets make visible statements about priorities. If the budget is pinched at the end of the fiscal year, some congregational commitments—utility bills, church mortgage payments, the pastor's salary—do not seem to be open for a lot of negotiation. But the amount we give to missions or to Christian education often seems more flexible.

For supporters of church schools, Christian education is clearly one form of mission. Since our children are not baptized into the church as infants, we have a responsibility as parents and congregation to nurture them toward faith. But the decision to follow Christ cannot be coerced. In this sense, children and young adults are an important part of the congregation's mission field. If we cannot find winsome ways of presenting the good news of the gospel to those who are closest to us—inviting them to faith and consciously nurturing them in that journey of faith—then it is rather presumptuous to think that we have anything to say to people whom we scarcely know and who live halfway around the world. In this sense, church-related education is simply an extension of the Sunday school or vacation Bible school program. It is an expression of Christian education that is already part of the fabric of the church's missional outreach. Others, however, are much more inclined to see congregational support for church schools as a kind of self-indulgent luxury: a potentially selfish act of spending money on ourselves rather than using it for "real" missions.

In response to these tensions, some congregations have tried to distinguish between internal and external expenditures in the church budget—or between domestic and overseas missions—and have developed formulas that keep these parts of the budget tied to each other by a fixed percentage or ratio. Thus a congregation might say that the level of its support for church-related education will never exceed the amount that it contributes to more traditional forms of missions. Other congregations avoid this question altogether by simply removing some or all of the financial support for church schools from the annual budget and instead creating a fund for designated giving to those schools. Those in the congregation who wish to support Christian education may contribute to it with designated dollars while the rest can feel good about supporting other forms of mission. Establishing a designated fund solves some internal tensions and may prove to be a good solution. But the principle of designated funds opens the door to larger questions about how congregations determine shared priorities; it runs the risk of establishing a precedent for creating numerous designated funds for a wide variety of individual interests that become disconnected from the larger vision of the congregation. As with all difficult decisions, congregations will need to communicate clearly, have transparent processes for decision making, and treat each other with graciousness and charity even amid deep disagreements.

3. If Congregations Provide Support (Such as Matching Tuition Grants) for Students Attending Mennonite Colleges, Why Not Also Provide It for Students Attending All Christian Colleges?

Some congregations provide direct financial support for students attending a Mennonite college or university, often in the form of a fund that matches a tuition grant offered by the school. Congregations generally look on this support for Mennonite higher education as parallel to other items in the church budget that fund churchwide programs. For students attending Christian schools that are not related to the Anabaptist-Mennonite tradition, however, this form of collective support from the congregation can feel exclusive: Does the congregation not value their choice to attend a Christian school, albeit not Mennonite, but one with a strong reputation for religious values and commitments? At the heart of these concerns is a question about the relevance of denominational identity.

From the congregation's perspective, the affirmation expressed by a grant to attend a Mennonite school is not for education in general—though members might think this to be a good thing. Nor is it support for a generically Christian form of education. Rather, congregations recognize that the denomination with whom they have chosen to affiliate—with its various program boards for mission, service and relief work, mutual aid, publishing, and education—exists only to the extent that church members recognize and value the work that it is doing on their behalf. Obviously, there are numerous worthy mission agencies seeking financial support; but Mennonite congregations will logically direct the bulk of their financial support for missions to a conference mission agency or to the Mennonite Mission Network. Likewise, there are dozens of church-based relief and service organizations; but congregations who claim the name *Mennonite* generally support Mennonite Central Committee and Mennonite Disaster Service. Clearly, private individuals in the church may contribute generously to a wide variety of agencies. But a church budget is an expression of a collective identity.

Consider this analogy. Imagine that a local Community Supported Agriculture (CSA) program might offer its members a 10 percent discount for fresh vegetables purchased at several local farmers' markets. A CSA member asks the organization to extend this benefit to vegetables purchased at a national chain grocery or discount store as well. After all, one could argue, the food purchased at these stores also has nutritional value. Yet, it would seem perfectly reasonable for the CSA to stick to its policy of providing the discount only to items purchased at local farmers' markets.

Congregational support directed to Mennonite colleges should not be understood as a moral judgment against other groups; it is simply a consistent consequence of the choice to identify with a particular group.

Addressing Tough Questions: For Administrators and Board Members

1. Should Our Schools Be Visibly "Mennonite" or Simply "Christian"?

Many MEA-affiliated schools were established in Mennonite communities during times of cultural upheaval, with the explicit intention of promoting Mennonite theological distinctives while also protecting young people from influences of surrounding culture. Church schools were a means of reinforcing the teachings of local congregations, especially as they related to distinctive Mennonite beliefs and practices.

As Mennonites assimilated into mainstream culture, these goals have seemed less urgent. As a result, especially in the face of pressure to increase enrollment, many Mennonite schools have begun to highlight the general "Christian" character of their institutions more than the distinctly Mennonite qualities. A corollary of this development has been a move on the part of some schools toward a greater emphasis on a missional outreach to non-Christian or unchurched families.

On the one hand, this could be seen as a welcome development. To the extent that Mennonites are participants in God's story, we share a great deal of spiritual DNA with the broader Christian church, Protestant and Catholic alike. No group simply creates itself out of nothing. Indeed, the Anabaptist-Mennonite tradition owes profound debts to the broader streams of Christianity going back through U.S. revival movements, European Pietism, and the Protestant Reformation. Beyond that, the Anabaptist tradition bears traces of the

Christian humanism of the Renaissance, the monastic traditions of Francis of Assisi and Benedict of Nursia, the theological writings of the early church, and the shared legacy of the Christian Scriptures. Mennonites today recognize that they are members of the larger communion of the Christian church and they desire to find common ground with brothers and sisters in Christ worldwide.

At the same time, our witness to the world is always embodied in a specific identity—in a culture, tradition, and community that takes on a distinctive shape and form. There is no Christian witness apart from its expression in particular, culturally embodied relationships that reflect a clear theological orientation. There is no generic Christian identity.

The Anabaptist-Mennonite tradition assumes that the good news of the gospel will always be expressed incarnationally and made visible in a way of life committed to following the teachings of Jesus, including Christ's command to love even those we may consider to be our enemies. It assumes that allegiance to Christ may sometimes be in tension with family priorities, economic security, cultural fashion, and national self-interest. It assumes that the church is not merely a gathering of individuals, but a living community whose disciplined life of mutual aid, giving and receiving counsel, and service to the world offers a collective witness to the Christian faith. These emphases are certainly not unique to Mennonites, but together they have given a distinctive character and coherence to the Anabaptist-Mennonite tradition for five centuries.

To be explicit about these distinctives can sometimes sound exclusive or arrogant. Yet distinctives of one sort or another are unavoidable, and these differences contribute to the larger mosaic of the Christian church. Schools affiliated with MEA should be clear that they are teaching in the Anabaptist-Mennonite tradition. No one going to Notre

Dame should be surprised to discover a clear emphasis on Catholic theology or the regular practice of the mass. No one going to a Jewish yeshiva should be surprised to learn that pork is not served in the cafeteria. Likewise, no one going to a Mennonite school should find it odd to discover a strong emphasis on service, peacemaking, or community. You might disagree with these beliefs and choose not to send your children to such schools. But distinctive teachings are the reason why such schools exist in the first place. So it is better to be up front, explicit, and welcoming about your identity than to be embarrassed, hesitant, or confused.

If we want to insist that Mennonites are basically the same as all other Protestant Christians—if the Mennonite distinctives are merely idiosyncratic quirks or cultural accidents—then there is no reason to continue as a distinct denomination. Indeed, it would be more consistent to dissolve the Mennonite Education Agency and drop the Mennonite name from our schools and churches.

Identifying schools as explicitly Mennonite may highlight aspects of Christian education that will not appeal to everyone. But this should be the beginning of the conversation, not the end of it. And it is possible for that conversation to move forward in a welcoming, humble, winsome way without needing to hide the fact that we have a distinctive identity.

2. Must All Board Members Be in the Anabaptist-Mennonite Tradition?

For most of the history of MEA-affiliated schools, this question was a nonissue. The great majority of Mennonite schools began through the initiative of local Mennonite congregations, with the assumption that those most deeply invested in the mission and identity of the school would be members of these supporting congregations. Though Mennonite schools have long welcomed non-Mennonite students and almost always included non-Mennonite teachers in their faculty, the board itself remained firmly Mennonite.

In recent years, this question has become more complicated. As a result of new missional strategies or budgetary pressures to expand enrollment, the percentage of non-Mennonite students has steadily increased in most Mennonite schools. Thus the question of representation at the highest levels of leadership inevitably arises. The issue becomes especially acute during capital campaigns, since individuals or groups who make significant financial contributions expect to have some ongoing voice in the long-term future of the school.

Boards and their supporting constituencies need to be very thoughtful in how they respond. They are the ones who ultimately define the school's mission and vision. Boards set priorities and communicate theological convictions through curriculum and policies. Perhaps most important, the board hires administrators and faculty who are the true carriers of the school's identity—they are the public face of the school.

Requiring all board members to be Mennonite offers no guarantee of a school's success. A healthy board will need to include members who reflect a blend of educational expertise, financial wisdom, theological rootedness, administrative savvy, and appropriate representation of various constituencies. Thus it may be wise to open board membership to a limited number of representatives beyond the Mennonite church.

But throwing board membership wide open is almost certain to have long-term consequences for the school's identity. If new board members do not share a commitment to the distinctive theological concerns of the Anabaptist-Mennonite tradition, it should come as no surprise when these commitments fade and other emphases take their place.

3. To Whom Is the Board Primarily Accountable?

It is crucial that boards of every church-related school give careful thought to this question of accountability. Sometimes board members think of their responsibilities primarily in personal terms. They were asked to volunteer their time presumably because they have already demonstrated leadership gifts, financial acumen, or administrative experience in other settings. So board members can easily react to difficult policy questions by offering their personal opinion, shaped by whatever experience they bring to the position. This is not entirely problematic— after all, board members should be free to share their unique gifts and perspectives. But at the same time, board members should not lose sight of the broader context of their actions. Their task is not simply to offer personal opinions. They are also charged with the larger responsibility of helping the school carry out a mandate and a mission statement that is bigger than any single individual. In this sense, board members need to cultivate an active awareness of their larger task.

The exact nature of the board's accountability will vary from school to school and will likely have both a formal and informal component. Some schools are patron run, with board members elected by parents or self-appointed by the existing board. Other schools were established by a regional conference and continue to be owned and operated by the conference. Most schools have boards with representatives appointed from a variety of groups, including pastors, contributors, alumni, the area conferences, or MEA.

One responsibility of boards is to be attentive to the various constituent groups who are invested in the well-being of the school and to thoughtfully balance competing interests that may emerge, especially when those interests are attached to large amounts of money. How does each decision shape the distinctive identity, vocation, or mission of the school as an expression of the larger Anabaptist-Mennonite tradition? How will people fifty or a hundred years from now judge the decisions the board is making today? What are the fundamental principles that will guide the board's work?

Church school boards face enormous challenges. Charged with the task of addressing the specific policy issues of the moment, they must also stay attentive to the dynamic realities of the local context and adjust to the changes in the broader social, economic, and cultural environment, while holding steady to the basic principles that give Mennonite education its distinctive character. Strong schools are built on the foundation of wise board members.

4. Are Mennonite Schools Places of Support for Students with Special Needs, or Are They Academically Excellent Prep Schools?

The easy answer to this question is both! Most schools that are committed to excellence in their work want to do everything well. Thus Mennonite schools should be places where all students can thrive and move forward in their academic, social, emotional, and spiritual maturity regardless of their beginning point. But when it comes to special services—whether it be remedial support for struggling students or extra programs for the gifted and talented—difficult choices almost always need to be made. Here a close look at the budget is probably a better indicator of the actual nature of those choices than the promises made in the marketing literature.

How one responds to this question may depend on the grade level and local circumstances in terms of available personnel. And it could be that there is no right answer from the perspective of Anabaptist-Mennonite theology. But I start from the assumption that education happens best in the context of diversity. Soon enough, young people will discover that they must learn to function well—whether it be in schools, workplace, or congregations—with people of widely varying personalities, aptitudes, and interests. Thus, to the fullest extent possible, teachers should aim at integrating all students within the same basic curriculum while adjusting to the gifts and needs of each individual.

When it comes to support, the tilt should lean in the direction of those students who are struggling. Care for the weakest members of the community—in this case, the academically weakest—is central to the biblical story. This surely has to be handled sensitively, recognizing that the identity of each student extends beyond intellectual aptitude and finding ways to promote a sense of community even while acknowledging significant differences in academic ability.

Providing adequate support for weaker students can be fraught with challenges. Unless church-related schools have a strong core of volunteers, for example, it is unlikely that they will be able to provide the same level of support for students with extreme mental, emotional, or physical disabilities as that offered in public schools. Moreover, the market pressure from parents is likely to tip toward gifted students—expanding options for advanced academic courses or increased opportunities for accelerated learning. No doubt schools should be as creative as possible in challenging academically strong students. But parents of gifted students should ask themselves what their primary goals really are: Do we want our children to have additional intellectual stimulus for the sheer joy of learning? Is it a race to graduate from college a year early? Is the goal to improve the chances for entrance into an elite school down the road? And how do we keep the current emphasis on accelerated academic programs in perspective with the emotional or spiritual development of our children? Would we press for an Advanced Placement course in "spiritual maturity"?

There may be a place for private prep schools that focus on getting their students into the best colleges and advancing careers. But Mennonite schools that promote their programs primarily to the academic elite are in danger of straying from their calling.

5. What Level of Facilities Should We Expect at Mennonite Schools?

Like all institutions, Mennonite schools need to invest in their physical plants. The environment of buildings and facilities and the surrounding campus all have an impact on learning. Campuses should be welcoming and warm and have well-kept grounds and freshly painted classrooms. Teachers and students can easily spend more waking hours at the school than they do at home so we might think of our facilities as a space in which we feel at home.

From the perspective of time, however, the significance of having first-rate facilities is likely to diminish. When older alumni think back on the truly formative moments of their education, they almost always recall individual teachers, personal friendships, challenging projects, or stimulating conversations that prompted them to see the world in a new way. They seldom recall the condition of the sports facilities, the quality of lab equipment, or whether or not all the computers were upgraded with the latest operating systems.

Our expectations regarding facilities tend to be comparative and contextual. As public schools replace cafeterias with food courts or develop new performing arts centers and gleaming gymnasiums, the pressure on Mennonite schools to upgrade their facilities in order to remain competitive is enormous. The same is true with church buildings, where our standards of aesthetic excellence and creaturely comforts have risen enormously in the past fifty years. Anyone who has spent time as a relief or service worker in a developing country is likely to marvel at the amount of resources that North Americans pour into buildings. Administrators seeking to raise funds for new or remodeled facilities must give a clear rationale for the need for construction and the significant investment of money that it entails.

In the end, schools should be simple, functional, and beautiful. They should be energy-efficient and multipurpose, serving as many groups as possible. Students and faculty alike should regard the space with respect and have an active role in its maintenance and upkeep. A visitor should not be surprised to see a student picking up a stray piece of litter on the grounds, an administrator pulling a weed from the flower bed, or a teacher painting a classroom closet on a workday.

Our facilities clearly matter. But we should not lose sight of the fact that finally it is relationships that make a community.

6. Are Conversations About Mennonite Education Irrelevant for Mennonite Congregations Located Far from Existing Mennonite Schools?

Mennonites in traditional centers of Mennonite populations can easily take the existence of Mennonite schools for granted. Yet Mennonite congregations at a distance feel as if they do not even have a choice regarding church-based education, at least for primary and secondary schooling. Why, they might ask, should we have an interest in engaging this conversation?

First, the question of Mennonite education matters to all of us because strong denominations require strong schools. Think about your next pastor. What kind of training do you wish for your congregational leaders? Even if your pastor did not attend a Mennonite seminary, think of all the books, periodicals, and curriculum material that would not exist apart from the Mennonite educational institutions. If there is anything in an Anabaptist-Mennonite identity worth preserving, then this tradition will need to be consciously cultivated, debated, modeled, and taught. This can happen at home, in worship, in Sunday school, in church camps, and in many other settings, but the most likely context for the transmission of a living tradition will be in our schools.

Second, all congregations can support Mennonite colleges, universities, and seminaries by including these schools in their annual budgets and by actively encouraging members to attend. During the past several decades, congregational support for Mennonite colleges and universities has steadily declined so that today little more than 10 percent of college-age Mennonite youth choose to attend a Mennonite college. Helping to halt and reverse this trend is an investment in the future health and well-being of the church.

Finally, even congregations in small communities or urban settings far from the centers of Mennonite communities should give careful thought to the possibility of starting a Mennonite elementary or high school in their areas. To be sure, establishing a new school requires a great deal of creative energy, commitment, and financial resources. But all the current schools began small. Every MEA-affiliated school has its own story of moving forward and succeeding against great odds.

New schools will not likely be able to offer all of the amenities advertised by the local public school. Yet a combination of vision, gifted leadership, a sense of calling, and a community of supporters goes a long way in turning dream into a reality. During the past decade, new schools have emerged in Philadelphia, Baltimore, Pasadena, and Hopedale, each reflecting a distinctive identity rooted in a local context. At crucial moments along the way, MEA staff have provided useful counsel; its staff remains ready to offer support wherever a new vision emerges.[20]

Addressing Tough Questions: For Mennonite Education Agency

1. What Is MEA and to Whom Is It Accountable?

MEA was established in 2002 after the integration of two Mennonite church bodies: the Mennonite Church and the General Conference Mennonite Church. To a large extent MEA continues the work of the Mennonite Board of Education and the Commission of Education of those two former bodies.

MEA is governed by a board of eleven to thirteen directors. They report to the Mennonite Church USA Executive Board, which appoints half of the board. The delegate assembly of the Mennonite Church USA appoints the other half. In addition, the MEA board may appoint two additional members who must be affirmed by the Executive Board. As an agency of Mennonite Church USA, MEA is accountable in a formal sense to the denomination. In light of its mandate to facilitate all levels of education for Mennonite Church USA, MEA's board and staff work closely with a wide variety of institutions.

2. What Is the Nature of MEA's Authority?

Altogether, MEA relates to over forty schools, including more than 14,500 students. These schools have a variety of relationships with MEA. The five Mennonite colleges/ universities and two seminaries of Mennonite Church USA serve their churchwide constituencies by relating to MEA through governance and advisory relationships outlined in separate statements of agreement. MEA appoints at least one member to each of the boards of the higher educational institutions; and for several of the institutions, MEA appoints the majority of the board members in consultation with the institutions. MEA seeks to ensure that the interests of the wider denomination are consistently represented in board discussions. Thus, for example, MEA plays an active role in the appointment of college presidents; it works to ensure that the colleges do not duplicate specialized programs; and it organizes regular conferences for faculty, administrators, and board members to promote a sense of shared mission and identity.

Schools from prekindergarten through high school are primarily responsible to conferences and other more local constituents. They participate in MEA through their membership in the Early Childhood Education Network or through the Mennonite Schools Council (MSC), which provides specialized services to the primary and secondary institutions it serves, and which has its own statement of agreement with MEA.

Ultimately MEA's authority, like that of most agencies in the denominational structure, is persuasive and informal, albeit within the structural responsibilities outlined in the various Statements of Arrangement.

3. How Is MEA Funded and What Does It Provide to Schools and the Broader Church?

In 2009 MEA had a budget of slightly less than $1 million. About 25 percent of its financial support came in the form of contributions from Mennonite conferences, congregations, and individuals, about 35 percent from member institutions, 15 percent from investment management fees related to the endowment, and the rest from investment earnings and other sources.

In general, MEA is charged with the task of promoting the vision and mission of Anabaptist-Mennonite education. The list of its activities is long. MEA provides support services during leadership transitions, continuing educa-

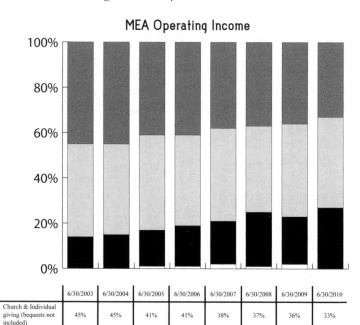

MEA Operating Income

	6/30/2003	6/30/2004	6/30/2005	6/30/2006	6/30/2007	6/30/2008	6/30/2009	6/30/2010
■ Church & Individual giving (bequests not included)	45%	45%	41%	41%	38%	37%	36%	33%
Support from institutions	41%	40%	42%	40%	41%	38%	41%	40%
■ Investment Committee/Other fees for services	13%	14%	16%	18%	19%	24%	21%	27%
☐ Other	0%	0%	0%	1%	1%	1%	1%	0%

tion through conferences, a regular electronic newsletter to strengthen the work of boards, and on-going seminars for new faculty members. MEA oversees a periodic youth census of Mennonite Church USA, and it brings churchwide educational leaders together for occasional consultations. MEA strongly promotes Hispanic pastoral and leadership education along with racial/ethnic leadership education programs and antiracism training. It also manages an investment fund for endowments and scholarship programs.

In recent years MEA has launched several initiatives to help its affiliated schools clarify their Mennonite and missional identity. The Anabaptist Learning Institute (ALI) is a joint program of the Mennonite Schools Council and Mennonite Education Agency. ALI offers teachers and educational leaders a series of master's-level intensive courses on Anabaptist-Mennonite faith and practice as it relates to the academic setting. In addition, MEA has recently adapted an accreditation process from the National Catholic Education Association called Validating the Vision. Elementary, middle, and secondary schools that are part of the Mennonite Schools Council have the option of pursuing formal accreditation with MEA. The process provides schools with an opportunity for a deliberate, structured conversation about mission and identity and helps to anchor accredited schools more firmly in the Anabaptist-Mennonite tradition.

Conclusion

This list of question and responses does not exhaust all the queries that one might have about Mennonite education. Nor do the brief responses offered here resolve the questions in a completely satisfactory way. But supporters of Mennonite education are clearly attuned to these tough questions, and healthy denominations are sustained by open and vigorous conversation. This discussion does not immediately resolve the congregational tensions my friend was facing about Mennonite schools. Yet such debates about matters of faith and practice are likely to be sustained in the future only if there are institutions to keep them rooted in a deeper understanding of Scripture and the Anabaptist-Mennonite tradition—institutions such as Mennonite elementary, middle, and high schools as well as colleges, universities, and seminaries.

6

Looking to the Future:
Challenges, Opportunities, Visions, and Dreams

In the fall of 1997, when a friend called Barbara Moses to invite her to leave a well-paying job with the School District of Philadelphia to become the principal of a Mennonite high school that did not yet exist, Moses had good reason to say, "No thanks!" After all, her position as director of social studies education allowed her to travel around the world. She enjoyed mentoring students and teachers, and she had even started to host a weekly educational television program. Moreover, the starting salary for the principal position was barely half of her current income, the new school still did not have a building, and Moses was not even sure who the Mennonites were.

Yet even after she had politely declined the invitation to apply, she could not get the idea out of her mind. "For about a month after I said no," Moses recalled, "the Holy Spirit would not let me sleep. I was miserable, crying daily, trying to figure out how I could live on half my salary while doing something I had never wanted to do." Yet her prayer was always to "be fully in God's will." In the end, the Spirit's voice became unmistakably clear. Moses accepted the position and became the principal of the first multicultural, urban Mennonite high school established in North America.

The origins of Philadelphia Mennonite High School (PMHS) went back at least five years earlier when a task force of culturally diverse Mennonite pastors began meeting to discuss the possibility of a establishing a church-based school in the city of Philadelphia. In 1996 a board of directors formed. Soon after Moses agreed to serve as principal, the board purchased a three-story school building on a quiet street. During the fall of 1998, the school enrolled fifty-three students in grades nine to twelve.

In the years since, the school's commitment to building relationships of respect, trust, and interdependence has made PMHS a safe haven and an educational launching point for hundreds of young people in the greater Philadelphia area.

In some ways, the differences between PMHS and the Greenwood Mennonite School in Delaware, founded seventy years earlier, could not be more striking. Greenwood was a rural school, composed of students and teachers who were all ethnic Mennonites, committed to preserving an established Mennonite identity. By contrast, PMHS is located in the heart of urban Philadelphia. Its students, faculty, and staff are racially and culturally diverse, and only a handful of its students identify themselves as Mennonites.

Yet beneath these apparent differences PMHS shares some striking similarities with Greenwood, suggesting that the newly emerging models of Mennonite education stand in deep continuity with the past. Like at all MEA-affiliated schools, following Jesus in daily life is central to the identity and mission of PMHS. Administrators and teachers actively nurture a strong sense of community, grounded in the Christian faith. Even before classes begin, all new students participate in a carefully structured retreat that highlights the qualities of mutual respect permeating the school's culture. From the outset, students are trained to T-H-I-N-K before speaking, asking themselves: Is it True? Is it Helpful? Is it Inspiring? Is it Necessary? Is it Kind?

PMHS students extend this sense of responsibility for community relationships by spending a significant portion of time in service. Every Friday afternoon, for example, PMHS sophomores volunteer as reading mentors, library assistants, and tutors in the local public school. Seniors focus their volunteer work in a line of work that interests them, serving in schools, community centers, businesses, and organizations. All told, PMHS students log over 10,000 hours of community assistance each year.

In addition to these structured settings for volunteer work, PMHS students regularly participate in cross-cultural and international experiences through an intentional program of field trips. As freshmen, students explore local educational sites in Philadelphia. In their sophomore year they travel somewhere in the state. Juniors take a trip somewhere in the United States, and senior PMHS students travel outside the United States. Already in its brief history, PMHS has sponsored student service and educational trips to Central and South America, Africa, and Asia.

Another expression of the school's commitment to an Anabaptist-Mennonite identity is the priority that administrators and teachers give to the skills of conflict mediation and reconciliation. From the first day of classes, students at PMHS are trained in the strategies and self-discipline of peacemaking, focusing especially on the peaceful resolution of conflicts within the school itself. The hard work has paid off. In more than a decade of the school's existence, according to Moses, there have only been four fights at PMHS, and none since 2003. Indeed, PMHS students are now called upon to teach conflict management training classes at a local K–8 public school.

"I hope that students will not only be successful, but that they will also be significant people," Moses stated, "that they will make a mark for Christ in this world, not just at PMHS or in Philadelphia. I want them to be great, but the Word of God says that those who want to be great must be a servant."

Through it all, PMHS faculty and staff have cultivated a deep sense of God's presence. "I wouldn't be here if it wasn't for God's call," reflected Pam Seretny, art and science instructor. "I literally start each day in prayer. One thing I've experienced here as a teacher is my own weakness and imperfection. But the beauty of being here is that when you feel this way, you know that God is truly at work. So I look at each student as an opportunity to allow God to use me, which is a privilege, and in a way that God is going to figure out. Because sometimes, quite honestly, I don't know what God's going to do or how I'm going to do it. But that's what makes it so incredible."

In an urban environment where violence, drug use, and high dropout rates are the norm in many neighborhoods, students at PMHS have a new sense of confidence, purpose, and focus in life. "They won't give up on you, no matter what," one young women reported about the faculty at PMHS. "They have higher standards for you than you have for yourself."

The story of PMHS is distinctive, but it is not unique. In 1998, members of the Wilkens Avenue Mennonite Church in Baltimore, Maryland, helped to establish the Mount Clare Christian School, which serves students in grades one to twelve who live in a low-income, violence-ridden section of Baltimore. More recently, the Peace and Justice Academy, founded by members of the Pasadena (Calif) Mennonite Church and cosponsored by Church for Others, a local Korean Mennonite church, opened its doors to students in a racially diverse neighborhood. "Our main goal," says Randy Christopher, who cofounded the school along with Kimberly Medendorp, "is to graduate students [who] will change our world. Our Mennonite tradition . . . has much to share with other Christians and non-Christians. An educational program that focuses on peacemaking and social justice in a nurturing community is a rare treasure and can be a precious gift to children and their families."[21]

The educational experiment that began with several ventures into Mennonite higher education at the end of the nineteenth century and then expanded to include elementary and secondary schools during the middle decades of the twentieth century continues to find expression today in new and exciting ways.

These stories of inspiration and hope provide a backdrop for some concluding reflections on the past, present, and future of Mennonite education in North America. In the midst of a rapidly changing cultural and economic context, Anabaptist-Mennonite educators face significant challenges. Yet there are also many reasons to be hopeful. Long-established schools continue to flourish as they creatively adapt to fresh challenges. And new schools, building on a deep legacy of Anabaptist-Mennonite education, lead the way in exploring mission-oriented models of education that will help the older schools adapt to new markets and new opportunities.

Negotiating our way with confidence in the future begins with a clear-minded perspective on the past and a keen understanding of the present educational landscape.

The End of the Institutional Era?

In the last quarter of the nineteenth century, the Mennonite Church in the United States was in serious trouble. The long bloody Civil War had not only divided the nation, but also left deep fissures within Mennonite congregations in both the North and the South. The lure of cheap land had prompted

hundreds of young Mennonites to move westward where
the small settlements they established were often widely
scattered and woefully short on leadership. Meanwhile the
heartland communities in Pennsylvania, Virginia, and Ohio
had been exhausted by a long series of internal divisions
that frequently pitted advocates for strong church discipline
and clear boundaries against champions of a more heart-felt
religion inclined toward ecumenical openness and revivalist
renewal.

Traditional Mennonite leaders found themselves out of
step with the assumptions of the surrounding culture. They
advocated a gospel of peace and humility in an age of chest-
thumping expansion. They spoke German when the future
was clearly English. They harbored lingering uncertainties
about commerce at a time when young entrepreneurs were
amassing huge fortunes. While other groups were establishing a vast network of denominational colleges, they worried
that higher education would lead to pride and acculturation.

By the end of the century, Mennonite identity in North
America could be accurately described as confused and fragmented. "If the young people go to church at all," wrote one
leader in 1890, "they go not to the Mennonite churches but
to others, where not everything looks so dead."[22]

Amazingly enough, however, in the following decades
the Mennonite church did not simply wither away. Indeed,
it survived and flourished during the course of the twentieth century largely because its identity was renewed by
the emergence of a host of new institutions that extended
beyond the local congregation. These new organizations—
larger than the local congregation, dependent on a broad
base of support, and focused on highly specific tasks—provided both a bridge between the Mennonite church and the
surrounding culture and a buffer that protected individual congregations from being swallowed up by the forces
around it.

The institutions took a variety of forms. Already in the 1860s, for example, General Conference Mennonites established a mission organization to promote outreach among the Arapaho, Hopi, and Cheyenne peoples in the Western states. In 1906 Mennonites in Indiana and Ohio consolidated several independent mission initiatives to form the Mennonite Board of Missions and Charities. In 1930 another mission agency emerged among Pennsylvania Mennonites in the Lancaster Conference. In 1920, five Mennonite groups cooperated to form Mennonite Central Committee (MCC) as a compassionate response to the famine and devastation of war unfolding in South Russia following the Russian Revolution.

Dozens of other institutions emerged as well. Women across the church organized sewing circles to support relief work abroad. Congregations pooled their resources to create mutual aid societies. Mennonite leaders responded to wartime conscription by establishing alternative options such as Civilian Public Service, PAX, the Teachers Abroad Program, and Voluntary Service units. Local conferences began to sponsor Mennonite church camps. In the wake of natural catastrophes, Mennonite Disaster Service coordinated voluntary assistance from across the church.

Each of these organizations fostered a greater sense of regional cooperation and shared identity through their efforts to carry out the Great Commission. They also opened Mennonite congregations to worlds far beyond their own communities, and they creatively channeled the energy of several generations of young people into the service of the church.

The flourishing of Mennonite elementary schools, high schools, colleges, and seminaries in the twentieth century enabled and sustained this larger movement. Nearly all of the early leaders of Mennonite mission agencies, publishing ventures, mutual aid organizations, healthcare facilities, and relief initiatives received some sort of training at a Mennonite college or seminary.

More important, these leaders kept the new institutions anchored to a theological and historical identity deeply informed by Anabaptist-Mennonite understandings. Thus, graduates of Mennonite schools composed and edited hymnals, biblical commentaries, devotional guides, churchwide periodicals, and Sunday school curriculum that shaped the spiritual contours of the Mennonite church in the twentieth century. The early explorations of Anabaptist history by Mennonite college professors like C. Henry Smith, Cornelius Krahn, and Harold S. Bender helped to recover a deeper sense of theological identity. The *Mennonite Quarterly Review, The Mennonite Encyclopedia*, and Bender's essay "The Anabaptist Vision" would have been unthinkable apart from the support of Mennonite colleges. The emergence of Civilian Public Service as an alternative to military conscription during World War II; Guy F. Hershberger's clearly articulated Mennonite social ethic; the highly influential writings of John Howard Yoder on the gospel of peace; and the thousands of books, essays, and articles published by Mennonite historians, theologians, sociologists, novelists, and poets in the second half of the twentieth century—all these are almost impossible to imagine without the existence of Mennonite educational institutions.

Add to this the hundreds of pastors shaped by Mennonite seminaries, along with the thousands of Mennonite elementary, high school, and college students whose lives have been transformed by their exposure to Bible classes, chapels, service projects, cross-cultural encounters, song-leading opportunities, and leadership training—and one begins to catch a glimpse of the long-term impact of church-based education.

To be sure, the role of Mennonite educational institutions has never been above critique. Mennonite schools have often been the sites of power struggles and church conflicts. At various points, some Mennonites have even regarded their church schools—especially colleges and seminaries—as a source of apostasy as much as renewal. Yet from the broad perspective of history, Anabaptist-Mennonite schools enabled the Mennonite church in North America to successfully navigate a tumultuous century of change.

By the beginning of the twenty-first century, however, the Mennonite church has found itself confronted with a profound paradox. On the one hand, considered from the grand perspective of history, things have never been better for Mennonites, at least in terms of their status within the broad family of Christian denominations. After more than four centuries of disregard or derision, church historians at prestigious universities now describe Anabaptists in respectful or even heroic terms. Although standard church history texts had previously depicted them as "the deformation of the Reformation," Anabaptists today are recast in many textbooks as courageous defenders of religious liberty and pioneers in the movement toward the separation of church and state. Thanks largely to the writings of John Howard Yoder, theologians and ethicists in both Protestant and Catholic circles now take seriously Anabaptist-Mennonite understandings of ethics and ecclesiology.

Today the distinctive theological themes of the Anabaptist-Mennonite tradition have entered into the mainstream of North American religious discourse, enjoying broad visibility across the denominational spectrum in Christian magazines and publishing houses. At the same time, the Mennonite church has found itself invited to participate in a wide range of ecumenical conversations in settings that would have been unthinkable in earlier centuries. This tradition, once reviled and persecuted by the broader Christian community, has now become a respected conversation partner and collaborator in many ecumenical mission, relief and service projects.

But this is only part of the story. Behind every silver lining is a dark cloud. Just at the moment when the Anabaptist-Mennonite tradition seems to have gained a new level of interest and respect in the public arena, the Mennonite church finds itself in a state of precarious health that may be verging on a crisis. Despite a recent merger of two large groups and notable growth in several urban congregations, overall membership in the newly formed Mennonite Church USA has declined during the past decade. At the same time, the average age of its membership has steadily increased. Overlaid on these demographic statistics are worrisome findings concerning core attitudes and beliefs. In 2005, less than one-third of Mennonites surveyed claimed to have a "very strong commitment" to the denomination; only 23 percent believed that it is "always wrong" to enter the armed forces; and even though 88 percent believe that "Christians should do all they can to convert all nonbelievers to Christ," only 18 percent do all they can on a "regular basis."[23] Nor does the litany of concerns end with these statistics. In recent years, nearly all Mennonite church agencies have struggled to maintain funding for their programs. Regional conferences have cut their program and staff to the bare minimum, and congregations have been wracked by the deeply partisan political divides that characterize the nation as a whole.

Despite some notable exceptions, a larger trend seems clear: many of the same institutions that had once been the source of church renewal and the carriers of Mennonite identity in the twentieth century now are struggling. These struggles have also affected the schools affiliated with the Mennonite Education Agency.

Contemporary Challenges for Mennonite Education

Economic Challenges: Keeping Education Affordable
As with public schools more generally, all church-related

schools are facing financial challenges. Over the past few decades, the cost of education has steadily increased, rising at a rate faster than inflation or income. At the same time, financial support for Christian education from congregations and conferences has wavered. Many schools have responded to economic pressures by tightening their budgets: reducing staff, cutting benefits, paring down programs, or deferring maintenance. Such measures run the risk of making the school less attractive to new students when pressures to increase enrollment are already intense. The challenge ahead is sobering: How do church schools continue to attract quality faculty and meet rising expectations on the part of students and parents regarding programs and facilities, while also providing scholarships to needy families who want a Christian education for their children? Parents face similar dilemmas. How will they pay rising tuition costs when employers are reducing their own healthcare and retirement benefits and when scholarship assistance is eroding?

The consequences of these new challenges are not entirely negative. In some instances these challenges have forced schools to ask legitimate questions about efficiency and accountability and encouraged them to become more innovative. In recent years Mennonite colleges and universities have broadened their offerings to include degree completion programs for adult learners and a new array of master's degrees. And as schools have shifted their recruiting and marketing focus to a more regional audience, they have asked healthy questions about the need to extend Christian hospitality to students from many religious, cultural, and economic backgrounds.

Other consequences of these new economic realities are more painful. In 2009 the Chicago Mennonite Learning Center, founded in 1981 with a vision of uniting Anglo, Hispanic, and African American Mennonite congregations in the greater Chicago region around a common mission, closed its doors due to a lack of funding. Mennonite colleges and universities are facing significant economic challenges. The states where Mennonite colleges are located—Indiana, Kansas, Ohio, and Virginia—have an abundance of church-related colleges with similar profiles, and competition for students in small liberal arts colleges is intense. Traditions run deep, and alumni loyalties are powerful. But there are no guarantees about the future. Indeed, some twenty-six colleges and universities in the U.S. shut their doors in 2007 alone.[24] The day may come when the colleges and universities affiliated with MEA will also need to soberly consider the possibility of structural realignments.

Changing Context of Education

Inseparable from these economic challenges is the rapidly changing nature of education itself. This is true at all levels, but especially in the postsecondary context of colleges, universities, and seminaries. Across the nation, the standard model of a four-year liberal arts residential college structured primarily for those ages eighteen to twenty-two is becoming less and less the norm. A growing number of students enrolled in higher education are adults who have spent a portion of time in the workforce and are now returning for focused training in specific areas that will supplement their career goals. Since many of these adults have families and are continuing to work, they are not looking for a residential experience, and their courses need to be scheduled in the evenings or on weekends.

In addition, the traditional distinctions between high school and college are also blurring as colleges face increasing pressure to offer credit for Advanced Placement courses or competency exams. At the same time, colleges are being forced to invest more resources in remediation programs and academic support services for students who arrive from high school unprepared for the rigors of university-level courses.

Perhaps the most significant shift in the educational landscape is being driven by new technologies. Thanks to technology, more information can now be delivered more efficiently, more conveniently, and more cheaply than ever before. New technology offers enormous potential for making education accessible to people of all ages and life circumstances through online courses, podcasts, and live-feed instruction. These new delivery systems collapse the limitations of geography and scheduling by providing college-level courses at times and in formats that are best suited for the consumer. But they also raise questions about the nature and quality of learning, the meaning of college credit, and the traditional importance of face-to-face relationships in the educational process.[25] Education mediated by electronic means is driven by disembodied relationships (hence the term *virtual* relationships). But if an Anabaptist-Mennonite pedagogy is truly rooted in the incarnation, then serious questions must be raised about the pedagogy of distance learning.

Market pressures are profound. When other institutions are offering low-cost credit via the Internet or degrees for purchase, church-related schools must communicate more clearly than ever why the margin of difference they offer is worth the additional cost.

Identity, Diversity, and Mission

Throughout this book I have argued that schools affiliated with MEA should actively embrace the distinctive themes of Anabaptist-Mennonite faith and practice and incorporate these theological convictions into the ethos, pedagogy, and goals of their educational institutions. If our form of Christian education is not distinctive in identifiable ways, then there is no reason for Anabaptist-

Mennonite church schools to exist.

Another central theme has been the recognition that students in our schools reflect a growing cultural, religious, and ethnic diversity. Whereas in the mid-1970s some 40 percent of all Mennonite college-bound students enrolled in a Mennonite college, today the figure has dropped to a mere 11 percent. Although the percentages vary from school to school, a similar decline in the overall number of Mennonite students has also contributed to this growing diversity. Part of the transformation can be attributed to a conscious strategy of mission: school boards and administrators committed to opening the benefits of Christian education to the broader community. But the growing diversity is also a consequence of more practical considerations: schools seeking to survive by broadening their economic base and appealing to a wider market.

On the surface the new context suggests an emerging tension. Identity assumes particularity and specificity. If administrators, board, and faculty do not understand and embrace the Anabaptist-Mennonite character of their school—not as a burden to be borne, but as a positive strength, woven into the school's very DNA—then there would be little reason to maintain an affiliation with MEA or to look primarily to Mennonite congregations for financial support.

An Anabaptist-Mennonite identity at its best is genuinely missional and eager to welcome, embrace, and learn from all students even if they do not share all of the same basic assumptions or convictions expressed in the school's mission statement. A missional identity and economic survival are not inherently oppositional. But Mennonite schools need to be clear-minded about the dynamics and consequences of this fundamental shift. Among other things, it suggests that the responsibility for communicating an Anabaptist-Mennonite identity rests much more squarely with administrators and faculty. It calls for a more explicit explanation of the Christian faith in an Anabaptist-Mennonite perspective. It requires greater sensitivity and respect for alternative, even oppositional, perspectives. It will demand administrative wisdom to balance the clarity of a distinctive identity with the pressures to become all things to all people in the interests of sustaining enrollment.

The twentieth century was an era of great institutional expansion. Mennonite schools played a crucial role in supporting the health, renewal, and transformation of the church. As support from the church for Anabaptist-Mennonite education wanes, MEA-affiliated schools will continue to adapt by orienting themselves more consciously around a commitment to mission beyond the borders of the Mennonite community. In both roles church schools serve the church by remembering and discerning our tradition of faith, and by passing along its essentials from one generation to the next.

Opportunities and New Directions: The Future of Mennonite Education

During the great age of cathedral construction in twelfth- and thirteenth-century Europe, the architects and stone masons who began working on these magnificent structures knew that they would never live to see them completed. Building a cathedral required the labor of many generations. Because construction moved so slowly, when work on a cathedral began, it was a common practice in many villages to plant large groves of oak trees, recognizing that ninety or a hundred years into the future, construction on the cathedral would have progressed to a point where sturdy trees would be needed for scaffolding.

Like planting an oak tree for a cathedral not yet built, investing in the education of young people is an act of faith and hope, a commitment to the future of the church on behalf of children not yet born. None of us can picture exactly what shape that future will take. The history of education is littered with the wreckage of new paradigms, touted by experts and consultants as the next big thing that eventually faded away. But even though the exact form of Christian education in the future remains obscure, we can prepare now to provide the scaffolding for later generations.

Every era of great challenges is also a time of great opportunity. Creative leadership for the future of Anabaptist-Mennonite education demands our attentiveness to a host of variables: changing cultural contexts, shifting market realities, new insights from research, and an ongoing openness to the movement of the Spirit. Without dreams and active imaginations, little of substance will happen.

Thus I close this book with a few considerations about the scaffolding that may support Anabaptist-Mennonite education in the future.

God's Kingdom Is Bigger Than Our Institutions

One initial step in dreaming about the future is to start with an appropriate perspective on our current educational institutions. However committed we may be to the well-being of our schools, we would do well to remember that the kingdom of God is not hanging in the balance of our institutional success. God's will and purposes in the world are bigger than the fate of Mennonite schools or the future of Anabaptist-Mennonite education. After all, church schools are human creations—they are intended to serve a higher purpose. Important though they may be, nothing about the survival of our educational institutions is divinely ordained.

This realization, properly understood, is not a form of pessimism, but a liberating perspective that offers the freedom to relax a bit, even in times of institutional crisis. It may be that, in God's providence, some things must die so new life can burst forth. A proper beginning point for all our thoughts about the future is the recognition that our goal is to participate with God in the healing of creation, not to preserve institutions we have created.

Embrace a Missional Focus

As we have seen, Mennonite education is in the midst of a profound paradigm shift. It is moving *away* from a primary focus on defending and transmitting Anabaptist-Mennonite principles to the next generation of Mennonites, and moving *toward* a mission-oriented identity committed to sharing Anabaptist-Mennonite faith and practice with students and parents from diverse faith backgrounds. Some newer schools have been operating in a missional mode from the very beginning. But for others, outreach to those who are not nurtured in Christian or Anabaptist-Mennonite families and congregations will require significant changes that are likely to be more profound than we fully realize.

If the identity of the school is no longer going to be carried by the webs of friendships, genealogical ties, and close congregational interactions characteristic of rural communities, then it must be nurtured in more intentional ways. This will require greater clarity about the school's mission, purpose, and identity and about its roots in the Anabaptist-Mennonite tradition. These convictions will need to be communicated intentionally and explicitly, not simply borne along by inherited habits and knowing nods of a tribal in-group culture.

Boards, administration, and teachers will need to engage their students with a missionary sensibility. At the outset of each new school year, we cannot assume that we fully understand the culture in which we are working. We will need to suspend our assumptions about the right way of doing things for a moment as a gesture of openness to the possibility that the Spirit will be incarnated in a new way. A missional focus means a genuine openness to the theological and cultural diversity that students bring with them, and a readiness to learn new languages, engage in cross-cultural translation, and actively invite the counsel of cultural inter-mediaries.

Seek Out New Allies

One expression of a missional approach to Christian education is a willingness to look outside ourselves and the Anabaptist-Mennonite tradition for wisdom on how best to move forward. If Mennonites in the past were inclined toward a posture of defensive retreat, suspicious of ecumenical movement as "watering down" the faith, Mennonites in North America today are beginning to engage in new, constructive conversations with representatives from other traditions.

Some of this conversation is happening in formal settings of structured dialogue. During recent decades, for example, representatives of the Mennonite Church USA have participated in ecumenical conversations with both the Catholic and Lutheran churches and, more informally, with Pentecostals, Reformed, and lay Catholics. The goals of the exchanges vary, but almost always they have resulted in a deeper understanding of our own tradition and a greater appreciation for God's presence in other traditions.

Another expression of Anabaptist-Mennonite ecumenism has emerged out of a broad, rather amorphous, renewal movement within the larger Christian church. The movement is diverse and goes by many different names—the New Monasticism, "the great emergence," the Third Way, the emerging church, and so forth. The various streams all have in common a high view of Scripture, a deep passion for following Jesus in daily life, a hunger for authentic Christian community, and a desire to place allegiance to Christ above all other allegiances, even if it goes against the grain of American culture. Leaders in these renewal movements are looking for resources that can help sustain them as they settle into more established structures. Not surprisingly, many of these groups are looking to the Anabaptist-Mennonite tradition as a partner and ally. They recognize the strength of connecting with a group that has a five-century tradition committed to radical Christianity.

What the consequences of these new relationships for the Mennonite church or its educational institutions may be is not yet clear. But at the very least these new relationships should provide resources for fresh perspectives and initiatives as we find our way forward as a mission-oriented church.

New Models of Education

Anabaptist-Mennonite educators in the future should also be in close conversation with other reformers who are proposing alternatives within the rapidly changing landscape of American education. Today, for example, parents in most states have the option of sending their children to one of the more than five thousand charter schools, which together serve some 1.5 million children. Charter schools can be created by virtually anyone who sees an educational need: Parents, educators, civic groups, business leaders, service organizations, and teachers can start one. Free from many of the rules and regulations governing conventional public schools, charter schools tend to be smaller than conventional public schools and serve a disproportionate number of poor and minority students. Yet they are funded with public money and are accountable to the state for educational results.

Parallel to the growing interest in charter schools is the homeschool movement. Although it is difficult to determine exactly how many students are being homeschooled, most estimates place the number at around 1.5 million. Neither charter schools nor homeschools replicate the educational mission of MEA-affiliated schools. But creative administrators might explore ways of collaborating with these emerging movements. Although charter schools do not have an explicitly religious basis, gifted educational entrepreneurs in a Mennonite congregation might take the initiative in creating a charter school, with the congregation taking a special interest in mentoring the students who attend. Perhaps Mennonite schools could make their athletic facilities available to a homeschooling network or offer them laboratory space on Saturdays.

And there would be other new educational models to consider as well. Given the fact that so few Mennonite young people are currently choosing to attend a four-year Mennonite college or university, MEA-affiliated colleges might offer a "Menno-term" that would cluster courses in Anabaptist-Mennonite history, theology, ethics, and literature into a single semester or during summer months, so that students attending state schools or other institutions could get maximum benefit from attending a Mennonite college for one term. Surely it would be even better for students to experience the community life and long-term relationships of a full Mennonite college experience; but attending even a few months with concentrated offerings in courses related to Anabaptist-Mennonite themes would be a big step forward.

In contrast to many other denominations, the Mennonite church has not pursued a systematic outreach ministry to students attending large public universities. Since it is not realistic for a group our size to assign campus pastors to all of these many schools, perhaps MEA could sponsor several professors from our church schools to serve as itinerant ministers and teachers, offering intensive, weekend courses in Anabaptist-Mennonite history and theology to interested students while communicating clearly that the church remains interested in their spiritual well-being.

Greater Cultural and Ethnic Diversity

One of the most dramatic transformations of Mennonite schools in the coming decades will be the growing racial and cultural diversity of our student population. Part of this change is an inevitable consequence of the new urban schools, which almost always bring a greater degree of racial and cultural variety. Another part reflects the shifting demographics of the United States as a whole. Today the Hispanic population in virtually every town and village is larger than it was ten years ago, and these trends are not likely to change. Yet another significant reason to expect greater ethnic diversity in Mennonite schools of the future is the rapid growth occurring in the so-called racial/ethnic Mennonite congregations. Whereas membership in Mennonite churches in the traditional heartland communities is stagnant or declining, urban Mennonite churches in cities like Philadelphia, Baltimore, Los Angeles, and Chicago continue to grow.

Officially, Mennonite educational institutions are all committed to the broader antiracism goals of the church at large. Yet the realities on the ground have often not aligned with our professed commitments. Transforming our institutions in ways that fully unleash the gifts of *all* our members will require a persistent and stubborn commitment to change. We will need open and honest communication, a readiness to engage pastorally with individuals who have been hurt by racism, and an ongoing awareness of systemic or structural forms of discrimination that can remain intact despite the best of individual intentions. Above all, transformation will require the presence of God's grace and healing love. One test of whether or not the Mennonite church has fully integrated the vision and energy of its constituent members can be seen in our language. When all groups can speak freely and naturally of "us" rather than of "us/them," the church will be a step closer to healing the wounds of race that have so long divided us.

A community of faith that has broken down the barriers of tribe, race, and ethnicity witnesses powerfully to the world. Mennonite schools of the future should lead the way in bearing witness to the reconciling presence of Christ in their relations with each other.

Learning from the Global Anabaptist Fellowship

Today, five centuries after its beginnings in sixteenth-century Switzerland, the Anabaptist-Mennonite faith is a truly global movement. According to the Mennonite World Conference, of the 1.6 million baptized Anabaptists in the world today, only 65,000 live in Europe, with another 525,000 in North America. The rest—more than a million—are part of the global Anabaptist fellowship, living in nearly 80 countries and gathered into 227 organized bodies.

As the numerical center of the Anabaptist-Mennonite church has shifted away from Europe and North America, the challenge of maintaining a sense of shared identity has become increasingly complex. Over the past century, the Mennonite World Conference has served as an important central point of communication. Regular assemblies have brought together many groups of Anabaptist-Mennonites from around the world for conversation, mutual encouragement, and the sharing of spiritual and material gifts.

Although the church bodies that relate to Mennonite World Conference differ on many cultural and theological points, all of them are interested in the question of education. The various Mennonite groups in Paraguay, for example, oversee at least eighty schools; and the Mennonite and Mennonite Brethren churches in the Congo operate some four hundred schools. Every group has a vested interest in providing basic education, training future leaders, and strengthening the theological self-understanding of laypeople.

When educators from numerous countries gathered for conversation at a Mennonite World Conference gathering in Asunción, Paraguay in July of 2009, the group had much to learn from each other. What sort of partnerships and collaborative initiatives might emerge from additional sustained and intentional conversations?

Clearly the dynamic growth of the Anabaptist-Mennonite church is now occurring among groups in the global South. Conversations about education would be a natural point of mutual exchange within the global fellowship and could strengthen, stimulate, and renew all of our efforts.

"Taste and See"

The themes of identity, crisis, and renewal are familiar motifs in the biblical story. The psalmist's words, "Taste and see that the Lord is good," offer comfort and solace to a weary people. "Blessed is the [one] who takes refuge in him," the writer continues, for those who fear the Lord "lack nothing, . . . those who seek the LORD lack no good thing" (Ps 34:8-10).

The promise of God's goodness and God's providence is not offered as an abstract hope or a spiritual ideal. God's goodness is not an intellectual or theological argument. No, the goodness of God is real and tangible. It is to be tasted, savored, lived, embodied, experienced, and enacted. To know God's goodness is to celebrate with God in the goodness of creation itself.

The incarnation—the Word made flesh—is the foundational reference point for Anabaptist-Mennonite theology and the basis for a Christian philosophy of education in an Anabaptist-Mennonite perspective. In the person of

Jesus Christ, God has risked entering the world in physical form in order to restore a relationship of intimacy and love that had been disrupted by sin. Restored relationships—with God, each other, and creation—emerge from the very heart of the good news of Christ's gospel.

Schools committed to an Anabaptist-Mennonite understanding of the Christian faith will reflect the qualities of an incarnated gospel. They will be characterized by an ethos of worship, an attentiveness to tradition, and the cultivation of authentic community. Their teachers will model the dispositions of curiosity, reason, joy, patience, and love. The true test of our teaching will be evident in our students through their growing attentiveness to God's presence in creation and in the full expression of all the bodily senses. An incarnational pedagogy will always resist forces that seek to divide spirit from matter, intellect from faith, or grace from works. Educators in the Anabaptist-Mennonite tradition will nurture in their students the capacity to recognize the healing hand of God in creation, the courage to participate with God in that restorative task, and the grace to recognize that we bear fruit only by remaining connected to the true Vine.

Medieval Catholic villagers planted oak groves, knowing that the results of their labors would not be fully appreciated for at least a century. What are we doing now to anticipate the needs of the church in the twenty-second century? Will future generations look back with gratitude at our wisdom, foresight, and commitment to generations not yet born?

Each day we experience God's gracious goodness. Each day we are called to witness to it and share it with others.

Taste and see that the Lord is good!

Appendix
Bibliography and Historical Notes for Mennonite Schools

The brief information regarding the origins of each school was supplied by MEA staff or by representatives of the school. For a complete and current list of schools, go to www.mennoniteeducation.org.

Primary and Secondary Schools

Academia Menonita, Betania, Puerto Rico
Date of Founding: 1947
Founding: No information available.

Academia Menonita, Summit Hills, Puerto Rico
Date of Founding: 1961
Founding: Summit Hills Mennonite Church founded Academia Menonita in 1961 as an extension of their mission to provide quality Mennonite education with English as the primary language of instruction.

Belleville Mennonite School, Belleville, Pennsylvania
Date of Founding: 1945
Founding: Local ministers who wanted to provide a Christian education for children in their churches founded Belleville Mennonite School in 1945.

Bethany Christian Schools, Goshen, Indiana

Schrock, Devon. *Hearing Our Teacher's Voice: The Pursuit of Faithfulness at Bethany Christian Schools, 1954–2004*. Goshen, IN: Bethany Christian Schools, 2004.

Date of Founding: 1954

Founding: In 1947, the Community Life Study Committee was formed out of Indiana-Michigan Conference with the goal to "carefully review the entire structure of our community life . . . and bring biblical and wholesome recommendations to our next annual conference." Among those elected by the conference to serve on the first Bethany board were Harold S. Bender, Amos O. Hostetler, and Guy Hershberger.

Central Christian School, Kidron, Ohio

Date of Founding: 1961

Founding: Various Mennonite groups from Kidron, Ohio—mostly within a collective from Kidron Mennonite Church—proposed the building of a Mennonite high school to the Ohio and Eastern Conference. Ground breaking ceremonies were held on November 26, 1959. This marked the beginning of the first Mennonite secondary school in Ohio. Central Christian High School opened in the fall of 1961 with eight faculty members, four support staff, and 156 students in grades 9–12. Clayton L. Swartzentruber, a minister at Chestnut Ridge, began as the superintendent of the school.

Christopher Dock Mennonite High School, Lansdale, Pennsylvania

Ruth, Phil J. *A Special Love: The Founding and First Fifty Years of Christopher Dock Mennonite School, 1954–2004*. Lansdale, PA: Christopher Dock Mennonite High School, 2004.

Date of Founding: 1954

Founding: Church leaders from Pennsylvania's Franconia Mennonite Conference introduced a questionnaire to area churches inquiring about the educational needs and spiritual nurture of their youth. The responses suggested a need for a Mennonite high school. The conference delegated a school study committee. A high school, however, was not approved. Congregations saw more need for Mennonite elementary schools and a middle school. Thus, Penn View and Franconia Mennonite were erected first. Seven years later, in 1952, original board member Paul Clemens again presented his plan for a high school, this time with success.

Diamond Street Early Childhood Center, Akron, Pennsylvania
Date of Founding: 1969
Founding: DSECC's ministry is to provide nurturing, safe, educational childcare that emphasizes the worth and uniqueness of each child in a Christian environment consistent with the Anabaptist mission of Akron (Pa) Mennonite Church. The center was started by church members.

Eastern Mennonite School, Harrisonburg, Virginia
Weaver, Dorothy J. *Eastern Mennonite High School: An Experiment of Christian Faith in Education.* (Unpublished paper, Mennonite Historical Library, Goshen College, Goshen, IN, 1967.)
Date of Founding: 1917
Founding: Plans for the school began in 1913 among Mennonite churches in the East. In 1914 at a meeting in Maugansville, Md., participants selected a board of education and decided on Harrisonburg, Va., as the site.

Ephrata Mennonite School, Ephrata, Pennsylvania

Shenk, Lois L. *The Story of Ephrata Mennonite School.*
Ephrata, PA: Produced by Ephrata Mennonite
School, 1996.

Date of Founding: 1946

Founding: No information available.

Freeman Academy, Freeman, South Dakota

Hofer, Marnette D. O, and Marie J. Waldner. *Many Hands,
Minds, and Hearts: A History of Freeman Junior Col-
lege and Freeman Academy, 1900–2000.* Freeman,
SD: Freeman Academy, 2000.

Date of Founding: 1903

Founding: As Mennonite immigrants from Europe began
populating the Dakota Territory, Friederich C. Ortmann realized the need for a school that would provide English subjects and German religious classes.
Ortmann slowly gained support from other Mennonite churches in the area. The South Dakota Mennonite College Corporation was organized in 1900,
forming a board of directors for future school plans.

Greenwood Mennonite School, Greenwood, Delaware

Bender, Nevin. *Our School, 1928–1959.* Greenwood, DE:
School, 1958.

*Souvenir Booklet: Fiftieth Anniversary Greenwood Men-
nonite School, 1928–1978.* Greenwood, DE: The
Greenwood Mennonite Churches, 1978.

Date of Founding: 1928

Founding: Greenwood Mennonite School has the distinction of being the oldest Mennonite elementary school
in continuous operation. It began in March 1928,
after the Mennonite students were expelled from the
Greenwood public school for refusal, on grounds
of conscience, to salute and pledge allegiance to the

American flag. Under the capable guidance of Nevin Bender, the congregation managed to keep the school alive even during the lean years of the 1930s. Greenwood Mennonite School is owned and operated by the Greenwood and Cannon Mennonite Churches.

Hinkletown Mennonite School, Ephrata, Pennsylvania

Date of Founding: 1981

Founding: In 1980, members of the nearby Weaverland Mennonite Church expressed interest in a Mennonite school. Hinkletown was established with the help of the Lancaster Mennonite Conference Board of Education. All parents sending their children to Hinkletown Mennonite School are members of the school corporation, which is guided by a board of eight trustees. The school is linked to the broader church constituency via a church-school relations committee.

Hopi Mission School, Kykotsmovi, Arizona

Esch, Andrew. *Dividing Lines in Hopiland: Hopi Mission School, 1951–1992*. Goshen College History Seminar Paper, Mennonite Historical Library, Goshen, IN, 2007.

Date of Founding: 1951

Founding: The Hopi Mission School was created by a group of Hopi Christian families that wanted their children to learn the teachings of the Bible. Before the mission school was built, school was being held at the Mennonite church in New Oraibi, now called Kykotsmovi. Parents asked Albert Jantzen, who was the pastor at New Oraibi at the time, to build a school for their children. A school was constructed in 1951 for twenty-six students. With the exception of the 1991–92 school year, Hopi Mission School has remained in operation since its inception.

Iowa Mennonite School, Kalona, Iowa

Yoder, Franklin L. *Opening a Window to the World: A History of Iowa Mennonite School: Celebrating Fifty Years of Iowa Mennonite School, 1945–1995.* Kalona, IA: Iowa Mennonite School, 1994.

Date of Founding: 1945

Founding: In response to the growing patriotism around World War II, Mennonites in Iowa petitioned for a religious school. Amos Gingerich, a minister at West Union, spoke out in favor of the project at the Southeast Iowa Ministerial Board meeting held at Wellman Mennonite Church. With the help of the MBE, a committee was elected as board of the new school.

Juniata Mennonite School, McAlisterville, Pennsylvania

Brubaker, Barbara E, David M. Brubaker, and Miriam K. Lauver. *Let's Reminisce: 30 Years of Christian Education, 1954–1983.* Thompsontown, PA: Juniata Mennonite School, 1983.

Date of Founding: 1954

Founding: Juniata Mennonite School was established in 1954 by a group of Mennonite families interested in providing a Christian education for their children. The Delaware Mennonite congregation made their recently vacated church building available, and the school was named Delaware Mennonite School. In 1980, a new organization formed whereby the school came under the direction of an association of patrons. The school's name was changed to Juniata Mennonite School.

Lake Center Christian School, Hartville, Ohio

Yoder, Elmer S. *Celebrating God's Faithfulness.* Hartville, OH: Lake Center Christian School, 1997.

Date of Founding: 1947

Founding: Patrons from five groups—Old Order Amish, Beachy Amish, Hartville Mennonite, King Amish, and Maple Grove Mennonite—were part of the group that started Lake Center Christian School. All patron members were potential board members, and the ministers who belonged to the patron body were at first automatically a part of the Religious Welfare Committee. The Amish not only enrolled their children, but they had direct participation in the governance of the school by board membership on a religious concerns committee. Twenty heads of households signed the bank note for $17,000. The school was originally named Lake Center Christian Day School. The first year they had 180 pupils, with five teachers who taught the eight grades and two high school classes.

Lancaster Mennonite School

Kraybill, Donald B. *Passing on the Faith: The Story of a Mennonite School.* Intercourse, PA: Good Books, 1991.

Good, Elaine W. *A School Grows in Donegal: The Story of the Kraybill Mennonite School, 1949–1999.* Mount Joy, PA: Kraybill Mennonite School, 1999.

Date of Founding: Lancaster Mennonite School was created when Lancaster Mennonite High School (founded 1942) and Lancaster Mennonite Middle School (founded 2000) and New Danville Mennonite School (founded 1940) merged in 2002. In 2003 Lancaster Mennonite School and Locust Grove Mennonite School (founded 1939) merged and in 2006 Lancaster Mennonite School and Kraybill Mennonite School (founded 1949) merged, creating the present Lancaster Mennonite School. It is known as:

- Lancaster Mennonite School–Kraybill Campus, PreK–8

- Lancaster Mennonite School–Lancaster Campus, Grades 6–12
- Lancaster Mennonite School–Locust Grove Campus, PreK–8
- Lancaster Mennonite School–New Danville Campus, PreK–6

Founding: Strengthening the Anabaptist roots and connection to Mennonite Church USA was a key factor in the mergers that created the present Lancaster Mennonite School. The mergers also sought to build capacity, develop a planned PreK–grade 12 curriculum, and to take advantage of organizational efficiencies. The merging schools believed that their common mission in Mennonite education could be better advanced as one new school rather than continuing as independent schools.

Lititz Area Mennonite School, Lititz, Pennsylvania

Date of Founding: 1978

Founding: Lititz Area Mennonite School opened its doors in September 1978 with sixty-seven students from forty-one families, representing twenty-three different church congregations and a teaching staff of six. The school began with a uniform dress code that is still part of the school today. A learning support program to meet the needs of students who struggle in learning remains an integral part of the program. The school's founders published a mission statement that read as follows: "The purpose of education at Lititz Area Mennonite School is to provide each student with an excellent academic background necessary to meet the challenge of the future and to nurture a firm belief in the Bible and in Jesus Christ as Lord in every area of life and to uphold the beliefs of the peace church community in the Lititz area."

Manheim Christian Day School, Manheim, Pennsylvania

Garber, Janice M, and Nancy Witmer. *Manheim Christian Day School 50th Anniversary History: 1952-2002.* Manheim, PA: Published by Manheim Christian Day School, 1991.

Date of Founding: 1953

Founding: In 1952, a group of Mennonite parents and church leaders concerned about the changes in the public school system started Manheim Christian Day School to pass on biblical values to the next generation. In the fall of 1952, the school opened its doors, holding classes in two one-room schools. The current location was provided through a plot of land deeded to Mennonites by Thomas and Richard Penn (sons of William Penn). In March 1953, ground was broken for the new school. On September 8, 1953, the school opened with seventy-nine students. Today, Manheim Christian Day School serves students from a wide range of denominations and continues its mission to instill education with biblical values, as the faculty and staff "educate minds, and nurture hearts."

Mount Clare Christian School, Baltimore, Maryland

Date of Founding: 1998

Founding: The journey to where Mount Clare Christian School is today began in 1997, when several members of the Wilkens Avenue Mennonite Church felt the need for a Christian school in their community. Many of the students at the middle school level were dropping out and falling into a pattern of delinquency. In 1998, several church members—two of whom were teachers in the Baltimore City Public School system—began to explore this vision. There were compelling reasons for wanting to start the school. The drop-out rate in the neighborhood exceeded 80 percent, with many students quitting in middle school. The local public schools were having a difficult time reaching the wide-ranging needs of their students.

New Covenant Christian School, Lebanon, Pennsylvania
Date of Founding: 1981
Founding: No information available.

New Holland Early Learning Center, New Holland, Pennsylvania
Date of Founding: 1981
Founding: No information available

Penn View Christian School, Souderton, Pennsylvania
Ruth, Phil J. *Sowing Seeds of Faith: The Founding and First Fifty Years of Penn View Christian School, Formerly Franconia Mennonite School, 1945–1995.* Souderton, PA: Penn View Christian School, 1995.
Date of Founding: 1945
Founding: A group of individuals from Franconia Conference founded Penn View as a Christian elementary school to begin their children's spiritual nurture at a young age. It became one of the first parent-controlled, patron-sponsored, parochial schools in the state.

Philadelphia Mennonite High School, Philadelphia, Pennsylvania
Date of Founding: 1998
Founding: In 1993, a task force formed and met with a group of culturally diverse Philadelphia Mennonite pastors. They presented an inspiring case for the need of a secondary school that would: (1) teach a spirit of reconciliation and peacemaking among youth; and (2) train youth to be contributing members and leaders in the church and community. In 1996, a

board of directors formed for the new high school. A search committee was soon brought together to find a dedicated principal to lead this new venture. Dr. Barbara Moses was chosen for her strong commitment to God and her church family and her agreement with Anabaptist beliefs. Her thirty years as an urban educator and her educational philosophy mirrored what the board had in mind. The board purchased a three-story school building on a quiet street near the Philadelphia Museum of Art in early 1998.

Quakertown Christian School, Quakertown, Pennsylvania

Date of Founding: 1951

Founding: Quakertown Christian School was established in 1951 as an educational institution of the Mennonite Church. The dream of the founders was to provide a Christian education option to prospective patrons living in Upper Bucks County. The majority of the founders were from Rocky Ridge Mennonite Church and the surrounding Mennonite community. Starting as a small enterprise, Quakertown Christian School opened its doors on September 11, 1951, in the basement of Rocky Ridge Mennonite Church with nineteen students from grades K–8.

Rockway Mennonite Collegiate, Kitchener, Ontario

Steiner, Samuel J. *Lead Us On: A History of Rockway Mennonite Collegiate. 1945–1995.* Kitchener, ON: Rockway Mennonite Collegiate, 1995.

Date of Founding: 1945

Founding: In 1943, the Ontario Mennonite School Board recommended to the Mennonite Conference of Ontario that they investigate the possibility of a Mennonite high school. A study committee was soon appointed by the conference, and classes began in 1945.

Sarasota Christian School, Sarasota, Florida

Date of Founding: 1958

Founding: In 1957 a group of twenty parents gathered at Tuttle Avenue Mennonite Church to discuss the possibility of a Mennonite high school in Florida. For the first year, Christian Day School was held at Tuttle Avenue Mennonite. Although all of the teachers and staff were from Tuttle Avenue, children from area churches attended.

Shalom Christian Academy, Chambersburg, Pennsylvania

Date of Founding: 1976

Founding: Shalom Christian Academy began as a result of the Christian school movement that took place in the late 1960s and early 1970s. Families of Mennonite, Brethren in Christ, and Church of the Brethren churches wanted to give students an opportunity to be educated with an Anabaptist perspective. Shalom opened in 1976 with a mission to assist "parents in providing a quality education from a biblical perspective with an Anabaptist emphasis." More than 60 percent of the students and faculty from this nondenominational school are part of Anabaptist churches.

The Peace and Justice Academy, Pasadena, California

Date of Founding: 2009

Founding: Members of Pasadena Mennonite Church began talking about starting a school in the summer of 2008. Their approach to education is based on the historic Anabaptist-Mennonite tradition of faith, peacemaking, concern for the poor and disenfranchised, and creation of genuine, compassionate community. Currently The Peace and Justice Academy operates from classrooms at Pasadena Church of the Brethren.

United Mennonite Educational Institute, Leamington, Ontario

United Mennonite Educational Institute, Leamington, Ontario: Its Origin and Growth, 1945–1975. Leamington, ON: United Mennonite Educational Institute, 1975.

Date of Founding: 1944

Founding: To compensate for the lack of private, church-related high schools that many Russian Mennonite immigrants coming to Leamington in the 1920s were used to, a Bible school, mostly focused on youth, was organized in the basement of Leamington United Mennonite Church. German language classes were soon added to the curriculum. As this program developed over the years, the need and interest for a formal school became apparent. At its founding, the first teachers were members of United Mennonite Church.

Warwick River Christian School, Newport News, Virginia

Date of Founding: 1942

Founding: Warwick River Christian School was largely the vision of George R. Brunk II, who had been a member of Warwick River's ministry team since his selection by lot at age twenty-two in 1934. Brunk's efforts were prompted by an emerging interest across the broader Mennonite Church to establish day schools for focused education of Mennonite children. The Denbigh Mennonites were encouraged by Isaac Glick, a key mover in launching Locust Grove Mennonite School in Lancaster County, Pennsylvania. On September 21, 1942, twenty-one children enrolled as the first students in grades 1–3 of Warwick River Christian School, which met in the basement of Warwick River Mennonite Church.

West Fallowfield Christian School, Atglen, Pennsylvania

Kauffman, Ruth L. *That They May Know God: West Fallowfield Christian School, 1941–1991*. Atglen, PA: West Fallowfield Christian School, 1991.

Date of Founding: 1941

Founding: West Fallowfield Christian School was established to partner with Christian families in educating and nurturing their children.

Western Mennonite School, Salem, Oregon

Lloyd, Melva Y. *Celebrating the Vision: Memories of Fifty Years at Western Mennonite School*. Dexter, MI: Printing by Thompson-Shore, 1996.

Date of Founding: 1945

Founding: Leaders from Pacific Coast Conference—Marcus Lind, Milton Martin, and G. D. Shenk—were appointed committee members to establish a high school for the Mennonite youth of their district.

Colleges

Bethel College, North Newton, Kansas

Wedel, Peter J. *The Story of Bethel College*. North Newton, KS: Bethel College, 1954.

Date of Founding: 1887

Founding: After past efforts of Kansas Mennonites to establish religious institutions of higher learning (Halstead Seminary, Emmental School, both in Kansas), another project began in 1887, when the Newton College Association (NCA) gathered with the goal of establishing a "nonsectarian but religious college." Early planning for Bethel College soon rose to the top of the NCA's list. However, tensions over religious direction and finances arose between NCA and the Kansas Mennonite Conference and threatened to stop the project altogether. David Goerz proposed a new policy that would appease both state laws and Bethel's intended religious direction, and a charter was signed in 1887, passing over the rights of the college to the Mennonite Conference.

Bluffton University, Bluffton, Ohio

[Members of the faculty], *Bluffton College: An Adventure in Faith, 1900–1950*. Bluffton, OH: Printed by Berne Witness Press, 1950.

Bush, Perry. *Dancing with the Kobzar: Bluffton College and Mennonite Higher Education, 1899–1999*. Studies in Anabaptist and Mennonite History 38. Telford, PA: Pandora Press, 2000.

Smith, C. H., and E. J. Hirschler. *The Story of Bluffton College*. Bluffton, OH: Bluffton College, 1925.

Date of Founding: 1899

Founding: After interest was expressed to start a college in Ohio, the Middle District Conference of the General Conference Mennonite Church appointed a committee of three, N. C. Hirschy, J. F. Lehman, and J. B. Baer, to begin planning. Although in the next few years the committees continued to fluctuate, the Middle District Conference, specifically with the leadership of Noah Hirschy, became the force behind Bluffton's formation (originally founded as Central Mennonite College).

Eastern Mennonite University, Harrisonburg, Virginia

Pellman, Hubert R. *Eastern Mennonite College, 1917–1967: A History*. Harrisonburg, VA: Eastern Mennonite College, 1967.

Date of Founding: 1917

Founding: Frustrated with the lack of a conservative Mennonite institution for higher learning in the East,

George R. Brunk, John Shank, Adam Baer, and Daniel Shenk from the Mennonite congregation in Denbigh, Virginia, circulated a petition to stir interest within the community. From there, a board was established and a constitution was drawn up. Efforts to associate the school with MBE were always met with criticism because of MBE's association with Goshen College and liberalism. Eastern Mennonite School was to be conservative and wholly under control of the church.

Goshen College, Goshen, Indiana

Miller, Susan Fisher. *Culture for Service: A History of Goshen College, 1894–1994.* Goshen, IN: Goshen College, 1994.

Date of founding: 1894

Founding: Originally founded in 1894 as the Elkhart Institute by Henry A. Mumaw and J. F. Funk, the school was not clearly associated at first with the Mennonite Church (although the school received support from Prairie Street Mennonite Church). In 1903, the school moved east to become Goshen College. Along with that move, the Elkhart Institute Association turned over its authority to the Mennonite Board of Education (MBE). New board members were henceforth elected by the regional conferences of the Mennonite Church.

Hesston College, Hesston, Kansas

Sharp, John E. *A School on the Prairie: A Centennial History of Hesston College, 1909–2009.* Telford, PA: Cascadia, 2009.

Date of Founding: 1909

Founding: T. M. Erb, a Mennonite preacher from Pennsylvania, was frustrated at the lack of a Mennonite Church school in the West (Bethel College was a General Conference Mennonite school, and Goshen College, although aligned with the Mennonite Church, was eight hundred miles away). By request from Mennonite delegates from the Kansas-Nebraska Conference in 1907, MBE appointed an executive committee, which later named and founded the school in 1909 as "The Hesston Mennonite School."

Seminaries

Associated Mennonite Biblical Seminary, Elkhart, Indiana

Preheim, Vern. *A History of the Formation of Associated Mennonite Biblical Seminaries.* (Unpublished paper, Mennonite Historical Library, Goshen College, Goshen, IN, 1960.)

Date of Founding: 1957

Founding: Associated Mennonite Biblical Seminary (AMBS) was a joint effort between General Conference (GC) and Mennonite Church (MC) denominations. In 1957 the Mennonite Biblical Seminary in Chicago (GC) and the Goshen Biblical Seminary (MC) joined together at the current campus in Elkhart. This cooperative effort initiated the formal link in 2002 to merge the two denominations into Mennonite Church USA.

Eastern Mennonite Seminary, Harrisonburg, Virginia

Reitz, Judith A. *History of Eastern Mennonite Seminary.* (Unpublished paper, Mennonite Historical Library, Goshen College, Goshen, IN, 1977.)

Date of Founding: 1965

Founding: Interest for a seminary in the East began at Eastern Mennonite College in 1921. J. B. Smith and C. K. Lehman were among the church leaders who pushed for the school to be established. The plan was accepted by the Eastern Mennonite College Board in 1958, and a one-year graduate course was offered in the 1960–61 school year. It was not until 1965 that the seminary was established with a formal name and a separate dean.

For a complete and current list of schools, go to www. mennoniteeducation.org.

Notes

Introduction

1. These figures are taken from "Fast Facts," National Center for Educational Statistics. See www.nces.ed.gov/fastfacts/display.asp?id=372.

2. In addition to those schools formally related to MEA, there are also hundreds of additional schools among other Anabaptist groups such as the Conservative Mennonites, the Beachy Amish, and the Old Order Amish. And several schools within the Mennonite Church USA constituency are not affiliated with MEA.

3. For examples of the Reformed approach see Clifford Williams, *The Life of the Mind: A Christian Perspective* (Grand Rapids: Baker Academic, 2002); Francis Beckwith, William Lane Craig and J. P. Moreland, eds. *To Everyone an Answer: A Case for the Christian Worldview* (Downers Grove, Ill: InterVarsity, 2004). For an ethnographic study of conservative Christian education see Alan Peshkin, *God's Choice: The Total World of a Fundamentalist Christian School* (Chicago: University of Chicago Press, 1986); and John Evans, *Clint's Story: A Public Schoolteacher's Case for Homeschooling* (Seattle: CreateSpace, 2009).

4. Two clear exceptions to this generalization are Daniel Hertzler, *Mennonite Education: Why and How? A Philosophy of Education for the Mennonite Church* (Scottdale, Pa.: Herald Press, 1971) and Sara Wenger Shenk, *Anabaptist Ways of Knowing: A Conversation about Tradition-Based Critical Education* (Telford, Pa.: Cascadia, 2003). Another noteworthy exception is Christopher Dock, whose *Schul-Ordnung*, written in 1750 and published in 1769, was the first pedagogical manual to be published in Colonial America.

231

Chapter 1: The Context of Mennonite Education in North America

5. For an account of the controversy, see Harold E. Huber, *With Eyes of Faith: A History of Greenwood Mennonite Church, Greenwood, Delaware, 1914–1974* (Greenwood, Del.: Country Rest Home, 1974), 88-103.

6. Interview by John D. Roth with David Yoder, September 28, 2009.

7. Donald Kraybill, *Passing On the Faith: The Story of a Mennonite School* (Intercourse, Pa.: Good Books, 1991), 9-11.

8. "Fast Facts," National Center for Educational Statistics.

9. Wladimir Süss, *Das Schulwesen der deutschen Minderheit in Russland: Von den ersten Ansiedlungen bis zur Revolution 1917* (Köln: Bühlau, 2004).

10. Kraybill, *Passing on the Faith*, 13.

11. These figures come from Paul Toews, *Mennonites in American Society: Modernity and the Persistence of Religious Community* (Scottdale, Pa.: Herald Press, 1996), 173; Steven M. Nolt has noted that these percentages may be misleadingly high, since some communities with larger Mennonite populations did not include in these calculations those men who had been assigned farm deferments as conscientious objectors. *Through Fire and Water: An Overview of Mennonite History*, rev. ed. (Scottdale, Pa.: Herald Press, 2010), 316, fn. 6.

12. Donald Kraybill, *Mennonite Education: Issues, Facts and Changes* (Scottdale, Pa.: Herald Press, 1978), 68.

13. Some schools, perhaps especially Bluffton University, had a high percentage of diverse students almost from the beginning. But these were clear exceptions to the rule.

Chapter 3: Creating Communities of Learning

14. C. S. Lewis, *Surprised by Joy: The Shape of My Early Life* (New York: Harcourt Brace, 1955).

15. For a helpful biography of Christopher Dock, including excerpts from many of his writings, see Gerald C. Studer, *Christopher Dock, Colonial Schoolmaster: The Biography and Writings of Christopher Dock* (Scottdale, Pa.: Herald Press, 1993.

Chapter 4: Outcomes of a Mennonite Education

16. "Fast Facts," National Center for Educational Statistics.

17. Miroslav Volf, *Exclusion and Embrace: A Theological Exploration of Identity, Otherness, and Reconciliation* (Nashville, Tenn: Abingdon Press, 1995).

18. In some ways "experiential learning" is an unfortunate label since reading, thinking and meditating are also real experiences, no less than an internship or short-term service.

19. Richard Louv, *Last Child in the Woods: Saving Our Children from Nature-Deficit Disorder* (Chapel Hill, NC: Algonquin Books, 2006).

Chapter 5: Keeping the Conversation Alive

20. See the Mennonite Secondary Education Council's *Handbook to Establish a Mennonite School* for useful practical counsel in starting a new school. Copies available at the Mennonite Education Agency.

Chapter 6: Looking into the Future

21. Laurie Oswald Robinson, "A Priceless Education," *The Mennonite* (January 20, 2009), 10.

22. Theron F. Schlabach, *Peace, Faith, Nation: Mennonites and Amish in Nineteenth-Century America* (Scottdale, Pa.: Herald Press, 1988), 295.

23. These findings, and many more, can be found in Conrad Kanagy, *Road Signs for the Journey: A Profile of Mennonite Church USA* (Scottdale, Pa.: Herald Press, 2007).

24. David J. Koon, "On the Brink of Disaster?" The John William Pope Center for Higher Education Policy, August 20, 2009, www.popecenter.org/news/article.html?id=2220 (accessed September 29, 2010).

25. Shane Hipps, *Flickering Pixels: How Technology Shapes Your Faith* (Grand Rapids, Mich.: Zondervan Press, 2009).

The Author

John D. Roth is professor of history at
Goshen College, where he also serves
as editor of *The Mennonite Quarterly
Review* and director of The Mennonite
Historical Library.

He is the author of numerous books
and articles on topics related to Anabaptist-
Mennonite theology and history.

He and his wife, Ruth, are the parents
of four daughters and are active members
at Berkey Avenue Mennonite Church in Goshen, Indiana.